Cardiff Airfields

Ernest Willows and Frank Goodden embark on their first flight from England to France.
November 4th 1910.

CARDIFF AIRFIELDS

Ivor Jones

Aureus

Cardiff Airfields is Ivor Jones' first book. It is the author's intention to follow this title with *North Wales Airfields* and *South Wales Airfields*. Further information may be obtained from the Publisher at info@aureus.co.uk or at the address below.

First Published 2003

©2003 Ivor Jones

Front cover photograph: ©Huw Jones. Concorde in all her majesty during a recent visit to Cardiff International Airport, Rhoose, Wales.

ISBN 1 899750 12 6

Printed in Great Britain.

A catalogue record for this book is available from the British Library.

Aureus Publishing Limited
Castle Court
Castle-upon-Alun
St. Bride's Major
Vale of Glamorgan
CF32 0TN

Tel: (01656) 880033 Fax: (01656) 880033
Int. tel: +44 1656 880033 Int. fax: +44 1656 880033

E-mail: sales@aureus.co.uk
Web site: www.aureus.co.uk

Acknowledgments

I would like to express my appreciation for the help and advice received from many sources in writing this book. In particular I wish to thank:

Captain Kenneth Wakefield (Cambrian Airways) for his guidance and patience.

Mr Ted Chamberlain, and Mr D Park (No. 614 Squadron R.Aux. Air Force) and No.7 Motor Transport Company. Mr Ted Williams, and Mr Goff Watkins of No.3 Reserve Flying School.

Mr John David (John Curran Aircraft); Mrs Dunbar, Mr Rick Moore, Mr Ken Rapson, Mr Sansom, and Mr C Burridge all of Messrs of Air Dispatch Ltd.

Mrs Iris Neale and Mrs Vera Cosh of 52 Maintenance Unit; Mr Viv Corbin and Mr Chris Taylor (Bruce Coach work).

Mr R Thursday, and Ted Williams (Cardiff Aero Club); Mr Ken Griffiths, Mr Terry Smith, Mr B T Macaleavy, Mrs T Green, Mrs Jenkins, Mrs Denley and Mrs Dorking all of No.1 Fire Fighting School (Min. Civil Aviation).

The Public Record Office, Kew Gardens, Cardiff Central Library, Glamorgan Archive, Western Mail, The Airfield Research Group, Mr David Smith.

'Action Stations No.3' published by Patrick Stephen, 'Twenty One Squadrons of the Aux. Air Force' by Mr Leslie Hunt; Mr D Elliot of the Welsh Assembly Government's Photo Unit, Mr Mervyn Amundson.

And lastly I also appreciate the word processing that was done for me by my son Barrie, and his wife Susan for helping out, when I hadn't the means or the ability to do the work myself.

Ivor Jones 2003

RAF Cardiff (Pengam Moors) viewed from the East overlooking the Rhymney River.

Introduction

Apart from the early flights from East Moors in Splott of Captain Willows, and then Charles Watkins, there was little to suggest that this eastern part of Cardiff would be the site of Cardiff airport, or aerodrome as it was called in the twenties and thirties.

Most of the airshows, and passenger trips used the Cardiff Racecourse, which was renamed the Ely Racecourse later, but when the tide fields of Pengam were fully developed in the early thirties, flying ceased at the racecourse.

There was another aerodrome used by the Cardiff Aero Club, and 614 squadron Auxiliary Air Force on occasional exercises, and by an Airline service briefly. It was in Wenvoe, a mile or two west of Cardiff.

On the arrival in Cardiff in 1943 and 1944 of units of the U.S. Army two landing grounds were established in the city to accommodate the small spotter planes of the artillery regiment based at the Heath Camp.

The move from Cardiff Pengam Moors to Rhoose on 1st April 1954 of all Civil Airline flying created another Cardiff airfield and is now named the Cardiff International Airport.

1910 - 1939

Ernest Thompson Willows - The First to Fly at Pengam?

Ernest Willows was born at No.11 Newport Road on 11th July 1886. A few years later the family moved to Dumfries Place, where his father had his dental practice. Ernest followed his father into the dentistry business for a few years, but it was soon replaced by his desire to fly. In an old shed on the East Moors he built his first airship, a fat cigar shape that was controlled in flight and direction using an engine and propellers. On 5th September 1909 the first Willows airship was lifted 120 ft. over the moors by Willows, just a short distance from the site that was to become the Cardiff aerodrome. On the morning of Saturday June 1910 the first Airship of Willows' design and construction flew from Pengam Moors to Cardiff City Hall. Only a few miles, but it was the first steps in the right direction. He was awarded a £50 prize by Viscount Tredegar. The Earl of Plymouth, Lord Ninian Crichton-Stuart and other notables were present. The airship was 74 feet long, a maximum diameter of 18 feet, a capacity of 12,000 cubic feet and weighed 650 pounds. It was driven by a seven horsepower engine.

On the night of August 6th 1910 he flew from Cardiff to London. It took ten hours and was the longest dirigible flight ever made in the country up until then; on this trip he became the first man to cross the Bristol Channel by air. On September 11th 1910 he flew over St. Paul's Cathedral and early in October demonstrated his airship at a large Japanese/British exhibition at the White City.

On November 4th 1910 he flew off to Paris in the Willows III watched by a huge crowd including Winston Churchill and David Lloyd George. He and his mechanic had a very long journey through fog over the Channel and it was 2 o' clock in the morning of Saturday, November 5th when they landed, 150 miles from Paris. It took him until Wednesday 28th December to reach Paris. The reason he made this trip was to raise the financial backing for his designs. He had failed to do this in the U.K. so his hopes were that the continent would respond to his airship. Unfortunately, the reason for his landing 150 miles from Paris was mechanical breakdown. Repairs were completed by the 15th of November and the trouble continued when the propeller shaft fractured. It was the 28th of December before this brave and resolute man flew past the Eiffel Tower.

1910 - Ernest Willows - Preparing for his first flight

He continued flying but was always short of money and no-one would give the backing necessary. The Royal Navy bought a Willows Airship in late 1913; he also supplied the War Office with two airship bodies and these were the only financial help he received. His airship was developed into two types of airship: a submarine escort and the famous 'Blimp' of World War One.

Mr Willows senior had financed his son's work over this period and was now nearly bankrupt, so Ernest accepted a commission in the Royal Flying Corps and he played a large part in the defence of London against German air raids. He designed a steel curtain which could be suspended from Kite Balloons. They were to hang at 10,000 ft, to protect the city from low flying aircraft. He was praised for his efforts, but there was no backing for his ideas.

After the war he fought hard for the financial rewards for his designs and hard work. In July 1920 he appeared at hearings of the Royal Commission on Awards to Inventors but the treasury hotly contested his claims. However, he was granted £1,000, an adequate recompense. In August 1926 in Kempston, Bedford, he was flying captive balloons at a fete where he was tragically killed. Four others died with him when the net ripped away from the gas bag, allowing the basket to crash to the ground.

Willows is buried in Cathays Cemetery, and his name is given to a street along side Pengam Moors Airfield. A school built on the airfield has also been named after him. The financiers were right not to back him, as heavier than air flying is safer and more efficient than an airship, but one cannot but remember Ernest Willows with respect as he had courage, industry and inventiveness.

1910 - Ernest Willows' first flight from Pengam Moors to the City Hall, Cardiff.

This is Willows School, built on the approximate area of the aviator's experiment.

Charles Watkins

A round the same period that Ernest Willows was building his airship on East Moors another Cardiff aviator was building his own aeroplane. His name was Charles Watkins. Born in 1885 in Cardiff, he earned his living as a motor engineer, but he became one of the earliest of the pioneering aircraft constructors with Verdon Roe, Geoffrey de Havilland and Tom Sopwith. The only doubt is whether or not the plane ever flew. In 1908 he rented a barn near Llys-Tal-y-Bont in Maindy, Cardiff where he designed and built his own aeroplane based on the Bleriot airframe, and the engine was based on the Anzani. It took eighteen months to build, and was covered in Irish Linen and was doped in deep red. He named it *Red Robin*.

Originally the plane was controlled laterally by wing warping, but he soon altered this to the fitting of ailerons. The engine was a three-cylinder affair, cast in aluminium producing 40 brake horsepower at 1,000rpm. The propeller was also designed by Watkins, and has the date 1908 on it. According to one witness, the first flight took place in either 1910 or 1911, but the whole thing is wrapped in mystery and doubt. Watkins claims that he flew, and several witnesses testify that he did, yet there is no substantive evidence that he did.

In the period around 1911 flying was still big news and his flight would have aroused interest in the press and public. He would also have been the first Welshman to fly. It would be the first Welsh aircraft designed and built, yet nothing was report-

Charles Watkins seated in his plane. He did design and build this plane though his flights caused debate.

ed. Challenges were being made around the world as to who had flown the furthest, highest and longest yet nothing was recorded of Mr Watkins' flight, from take off on the moors, across Whitchurch to Caerphilly Mountain and back to East Moor. One witness claims to have seen the red monoplane over Cardiff Docks.

The plane had never been registered, and Watkins had not obtained a pilot's licence. In 1916 one of the cylinder heads cracked and grounded the plane. No one knows if it did or did not fly again after that date.

Charles Watkins' 'Red Robin' hangs aloft in the National Museum of Wales, Cardiff.

It was stored in his garage at Colum Road in Cardiff until 1943 when it was a re-assembled and exhibited at a 'Wings for Victory' appeal in Cardiff. In 1945 Watkins offered it to the National Museum of Wales, but he was not happy about the way they wished to display it, so it remained in his garage. A few years later it was spotted by an R.A.F. officer, who persuaded Watkins to contribute his aircraft to the St. Athan Museum of Flight. Mr Watkins re-assembled 'Red Robin' and it was on display in a hangar at the R.A.F. station at St Athan until 1961-62. The airframe was in mint condition, but the fabric had to be replaced with Egyptian cotton, and they fitted new wheels.

The plane stayed at the museum from then until the St. Athan collection was dispersed by Air Ministry orders to the R.A.F. Museums at Hendon and Cosford around 1990.

Red Robin is now suspended high up in the hall of The National Museum of Wales at Cathays Park, Cardiff.

Mr Watkins did not finish with aviation after building Red Robin but claims to have worked with A.V. Roe for a few years before the outbreak of World War One. Watkins died in 1970 aged 91, undoubtedly an excellent engineer, and the first Welshman to design and build and *perhaps* fly his own aircraft from Welsh soil.

Ely Racecourse

While the experiments with airship and airplane had been proceeding at Pengam Moors to the east of Cardiff, another place was entertaining the public with the new thrill of aviation. It was to the west of the city at the well-known Cardiff Racecourse, later named Ely Racecourse. Air displays or exhibitions as they were called then, were held at Ely before World War One. Gustav Hamel would thrill spectators with aerobatics in his Morane Saulnier. Hamel was famous and on 9th September

This 1946 RAF shot only shows the area. The racetrack has been demolished.
Parts of the Grandstand and Enclosures remain (right of centre). Courtesy of the Welsh Assembly.

Gustav Hamel at Ely Racecourse in 1913. He died a year later.

1911, carried the first official Air Mail from Hendon to Windsor. His career was cut short in May 1914, when his plane ditched in the English Channel.

Another aviation pioneer was David Prosser who also visited Ely racecourse. He obtained his pilot' certificate (No.526) from the Royal Aero Club on 18th June 1913, flying a Caudron. These men were in the forefront of aviation even before the huge advances that World War One was about to bring.

On 22nd September 1911 the Western Mail reported that history was made at Ely racecourse in Cardiff on Saturday, and it is difficult to foresee the far-reaching results of what took place! (It was reporting on the item that follows); 'Mr.Grindell-Matthews, the inventor of the AERO-PHONE succeeded under the most trying conditions in establishing a communications by wireless telephony with an 'aeroplanist' careering in

Edwin Prosser at Ely in 1913 with his Caudron.

Mr B.C. Hucks in his aircraft 'Mercury' on Ely Racecourse testing Grindell-Matthews' aerophone.
September 1911.

the air 700ft. high, in strong winds and heavy rain, and at the speed of an express train!

The most sanguine hopes of the experts on the ground were more than realised and the inventor went away pleased. Mr. B.C. Hucks, the plucky young aviator who braved the elements under conditions the majority of flying men would have deemed too dangerous, is also pleased to be the first airman to take part in wireless telephony. His fine Blackburn monoplane, the Mercury acted splendidly in the tricky wind, and when he descended with the telephone receivers still tied around his head, he was given a hearty cheer.'

Grindell-Matthews operating the ground set of the aerophone on Ely Racecourse.
September 22, 1911.

An advertisement for Imperial Airways Airliner at Ely Racecourse, 29 April 1931.

Two months previously Ely had a grand flying week, with passengers enjoying flights at £1.10 return. The exuberant Western Mail reporter took his first flight and stated that an interesting feature of the flight was the filming of the whole thing by the Gaumont Film Company.

At the end of World War One many businessmen could see the advantages of air travel, and one of these was Captain Alfred Instone. He was the vice chairman of S. Instone and Co. a large shipping company that, among other things, shipped vast cargoes of coal from Cardiff to ports on the continent, and the early arrival of documents of lading to the ports on the receiving end saved time and money. Alfred describes all this in his history of the company; 'We had a fleet of steamers, both our own, and time chartered, which were costing us a lot of money each day, and it was

The 'City of Cardiff' operated for Instone Airline from Ely Racecourse
(note the name on the engine cowling).

Instone Airline. Captain Barnard pilots the first flight to the continent for the company at Hounslow. 13th October 1919.

quite customary for these ships to arrive at north French ports a week or ten days before they could discharge their cargoes, owing to the fact that the bills of lading were delayed in the post. These were mostly cargoes of Welsh coal at this time.

'We conceived the idea of purchasing an aeroplane and getting the Government's permission to carry our own letters, which was granted, with the result that after our ships were loaded with coal the documents were sent over by plane, and the ships were consequently in a position to proceed to their berths, and discharge their cargoes immediately on arrival – perhaps a week before other vessels forced to lie off ports awaiting the documents to arrive. This was the means of saving the company thousands of pounds in ship hire and demurrage. Out of this arose Instone Airline as a separate entity to its parent.

'Our first aeroplane was a two-seater D.H.4 with a Rolls-Royce engine, and in October 1919 Barnard took it on its first flight to Cardiff. It returned with documents to Hounslow London in 56 mins. And soon after left on its first trip to Paris. The D.H.4 was an ex-war plane with the pilot occupying an open cockpit, and two passengers could be carried in an enclosed cabin behind him.

This flight was not the first connection of the name of Instone with aviation. As long ago as August 1910 the company promoted the flight of Willow's airship 'City of Cardiff' on a similar trip to London. This airline prospered and expanded, and was absorbed in to the mighty Imperial Airways in 1924 and the flights from Ely Racecourse ceased.

When Cardiff Corporation decided to Town Plan their area, one of the proposals in the forefront of the scheme was provision of an aerodrome, and in 1921 the racecourse at Ely was earmarked for the purpose, and embodied in the Town Planning scheme as an open space.

In 1927 the matter of an aerodrome became a practical policy, but it was found that that this particular land was not suitable owing to its configuration around the actual racetrack. Other sites were therefore carefully examined, and finally the Splott foreshore, generally known as Pengam Moor was decided upon. On choosing this site the Corporation were influenced by the fact that, immediately adjoining, it would be possible to develop, at little expense, a similar accommodation for seaplanes. A most desirable combination. It only remained to purchase the land at Pengam.

Acquisition of lands for Splott Aerodrome

Lord Tredegar was the largest owner of land in this region of Cardiff with 919 acres compared to the next largest, the Marquis of Bute's 64 acres. Pengam Farm was the second biggest farm in the parish and formed part of the Tredegar estate. The land is the area bounded to the north by the G.W.R. (Great Western Railway) main line, to the east by the river Rhymney, to the west by Roath branch railway to the docks at Roath dock owned by the Taff Vale Railway Co., and to the south by the River Severn/Bristol Channel.

This was moorland grazed by the sheep of Pengam, with no access to the sea from inland without trespass. The Cardiff Corporation leased almost all the land from the Tredegar estate for tipping and only occasional brushes with the legal side of the city and Tredegar exist. Three small irritations were over little things like the locals trespassing on to the foreshore in the their leisure time, but of much more financial importance were the efforts to repair the inroads of the sea at the original sea wall.

The high tides and storms were continually eroding the East Moor and Pengam Moor coastline and the ratepayers of Cardiff had to pay for the repairs, because though it was Tredegar's land, he was not responsible for its flooding or the fight to stop it, in law anyway. The estate and city compromised over this in later years, and while the City Engineers built a strong sea wall, the resulting expense was shared by the Lord Tredegar's estate.

From that period on the Cardiff Corporation ceased to ignore the area of moorland and slowly came to the conclusion it would be wise to purchase it all, and use it for leisure purposes. This affinity with leisure and fresh air exercise was a fine thing and the city had a good parks sub-committee. The inspiration was probably the gift from Lord Tredegar in December 1901, of 18 acres of land to build Splott park . The only expense to the city from this was to recompense the farmer William Williams of Splott farm to give up possession. The gentleman was pleased to accept 270 pounds i.e. 18 acres at 15 pounds each = 270 pounds. Mr. H.J. Davies was the agent for the Tredegar estate at the time.

To give an idea how a problem with keeping the sea away from the land at the foreshore slowly develops into the Cardiff Corporations creating and owning an aerodrome, the following negotiations are worth considering:

Public Works and Parks Sub-Committee 4th May 1925.

Land at Splott

A letter dated 9th April was read from the agent of the Tredegar estates, stating that he was prepared to advise a sale of the freehold of this land to Cardiff Corporation subject to the approval of Lord Tredegar and his trustees and to a valuation. The valuation was

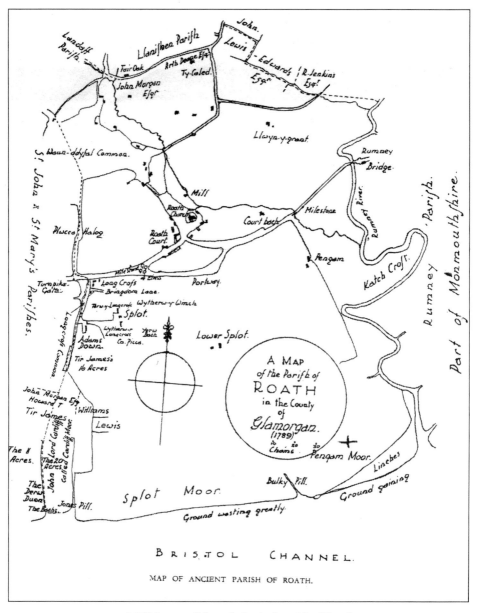

A 1789 map of the ecclesiastical parish of Roath.

to be prepared by the valuer appointed by them, whose fees the Corporation would be expected to pay whether a sale would be made or not. One of the conditions of this valuation would be that the estate reserve the right of railway access at any time across the land proposed to be acquired of access to Lord Tredegar's land adjoining. Subject also in the event of the sale proceeding, to the Corporation paying the estates legal and other charges in connection to the sale.

Resolved
1. That the terms of the letter (above) be agreed to, but that the estate be desired to sell the whole of their land situation to the south of the sea bank and west of the Rhymney river, but including the land now leased from them for tipping purposes on both sides of the sea bank.
2. That the City Engineer prepare a plan showing the proposals of this sub-committee, and that a copy of the plan in so far as it affects the Tredegar estates be forwarded to Lord Tredegar's agent.

Foreshore – A letter was received from the Board of Trade asking for what purpose the Corporation desired to purchase the tidal lands.

Resolved
1. That the Board of Trade be informed that the Corporation require the lands for the purpose of public recreation.
2. That the chairman, Councillor Thomas Williams and the Town Clerk be appointed a deputation to interview the Board of Trade in relation to the whole matter.

Meeting of sub-committee 8th October 1925
A letter from the agent of Tredegar estates suggesting the Corporation making an offer for the lands at Splott.

Resolved
That the town Clerk be authorised to engage the services of a valuer and the result be reported to the sub-committee as soon as possible.

Meeting of Public Works and Parks Joint Sub-Committee 17th May 1926
Splottlands – A confidential interim report upon this land was received from the valuer. The City Engineer reported on the most convenient line of access to the land from Newport Road.
Resolved – That subject to the approval of the finance committee it be a recommendation to the council to negotiate with the Tredegar estate for the purchase of the land now rented from the estate for tipping purposes.

Public Works and Parks Joint Sub-Committee 27th May 1927

Resolved – That committee proceed with negotiations to acquire the lands comprised in the lease to the Corporation and also the small plots of land belonging to other owners edged yellow and pink on the plan surrounded by the land compromised in the lease.

17th April 1929

A letter from the Secretary in Incorporated Chamber of Commerce. With regard to the development of commercial aviation, and that Cardiff should not lag behind in this respect and consideration be given to the question of aerial facilities to and from Cardiff.

Committee Meeting June 1930

A letter was received from the Air Ministry as follows, 'I am commanded by the Air Council to refer to previous correspondence ending with your letter of 4th June (C.S.) relative to the proposed establishment and maintenance of a Municipal aerodrome and the acquisition of land for that purpose at Splott Cardiff. I am to inform you that the council hereby give their consent to the proposal as required by section 8 of the Air Navigation Act 1920, subject to the condition that before use an aerodrome, the site shall be inspected and approved by the Air Ministry for the issue of an aerodrome licence, for use is enclosed.'

The Town Clerk reports 1st December 1930

That completion of purchase of freehold lands at Splott. From: Tredegar estates; Mountjoy Ltd; Roath Court estate; Lee estate and Mackworth estate there remained only the conveyancing of the foreshore.

30th April 1931

The City Engineer is authorised to inspect other aerodromes to see the layout of the sites.

May 1931

Aerodrome site: Cardiff Flying Club

A deputation consisting of: Capt. Bailey; Mr.S.C..Keene; R.J.Richards and J.P.&H.M. Ingledew representing the proposed Cardiff Flying Club attended and asked the committee if they would give the proposed club permission to use the site and the right of use of a piece of land with a hangar and other buildings to be erected by the Corporation.

The deputation explained that the club would be a private company and its objects would be to endeavour to develop flying in the city by teaching persons to fly and the supplying of Air Taxis and to encourage aircraft to come to Cardiff. If satisfactory arrangements could be made then the club could undertake to manage the aerodrome both from the sporting and commercial aspects until such time as the Corporation might decide to enter into an arrangement with a commercial aviation company, when the club would cease to take any part in connection with that side of flying, but they asked that the club should be allowed to continue to have the use of the land and buildings granted them and also the right to take off and land at the aerodrome.

Resolved
1. That this committee agree in principle with the suggestion of the deputation, subject to an agreement being entered into between the Corporation and the proposed flying club satisfactory to this committee and the Corporation. It was also agreed that a sub-committee comprising: Chairman; Deputy Chairman Alderman Charles; Councillors Hiles and Shippobotham, together with the Town Clerk and the City Engineer, be appointed to confer further with the members of the deputation to draw up terms for an agreement.
2. That the Finance Committee and the Council be asked for a sum of money not exceeding 1,000 pounds for the purpose of providing a hangar and apron on the aerodrome site.

The Municipal Aerodrome was born and land acquisition had faded from the minds of the Corporation Airport Committee until August 19th 1936 when the first signs of re-armament were emerging.

While the negotiations were going on at the City Hall over Pengam Moors, and occasional flying took place at Ely Racecourse, another airfield in Cardiff was in steady use at Wenvoe.

Situated 4 miles west of Cardiff town centre, just south of the A48 at the Tumble Hill, a few hundred yards from the pleasant hamlet of Twyn-yr-Odyn lies Wenvoe Aerodrome.

Cardiff flying club first used the field on the first of August 1931 on the undulating grassy area known as St. Lythans Down, a sum of 26 acres in area. They installed one wooden hangar and three small corrugated steel hangars. A club house (a redundant railway coach) a workshop and a fuel tank were also built and were all located in the south east corner of the field alongside the reservoir located in the next field.

It was just used for club flying for a while, then other aviation interests began to look at the site, as Pengam Moor was not yet complete. In January 1932 the Bristol Evening News attempted a regular Bristol to Cardiff cross channel service. Twice daily they operated with an Avro 10 (two crew and eight passengers) chartered from Imperial Airways, but it was not commercially viable and ceased after only one week.

On 10th July 1934 a licence for one year was issued to South Wales Airways Ltd whom had plans to expand the airfield. The licence was renewed a year later in 1935 but the following year they were denied. The Air Ministry Inspectors said that a new licence would only be renewed if certain improvements to the actual landing surface

Wenvoe Aerodrome is shown inside the dotted lines. It now has a TV mast at its centre.
Courtesy Welsh Assembly.

were made, the main problem being a slight mound in the flight path, no matter in which direction a pilot chose. That same mound is the very spot on which Wenvoe television mast is built. In those days of non-mechanisation it would not have been feasible to remove this mound and other projects as required by the Air Ministry.

So the years went by with private illegal landings at the site, especially when Pengam Moors was flooded. The site owner was disgusted and complained to the Air Ministry, stating that a fully laden Armstrong Whitworth Argosy and three R.A.F. Hawker Audax carrying senior R.A.F. Officers had used the airfield, he used the argument 'What's good enough for the R.A.F. should be good enough for other flyers, so licence me!'

Then in December 1938 the Straight Corporation applied for a temporary licence to use Wenvoe as the terminal for the cross channel (Bristol) scheduled service whenever Pengam Moors was unusable.

They were granted a one month's licence on the 23rd December on the proviso that rescue equipment and a wind sock were installed. The licence was renewed several times during the early part of 1939. Use of Wenvoe was restricted to D.H. 84 Dragon aircraft in low wind conditions.

On 1st February South Wales Airways objected to the licence being issued to The Straight Corporation and the Air Ministry said there was no question of a permanent licence being issued to anyone.

In March the Cardiff Aeroplane Club, also victims of Pengam Moors' waterlogged surface asked the Air Ministry for permission to use Wenvoe for circuits and bumps but no response was ever recorded. The last temporary licence was issued in June 1939, by which time Pengam Moors was fully serviceable and Wenvoe passed into history. The runways were: from North to South, a maximum length of 1,500 feet and East to West 1,350 feet.

Mr Bill Greatrex, who is now in his late seventies, helped me to view the airfield. Except for the T.V. mast the fields are much as they were when he was a lad in the thirties. He recalls 'Alan Cobham's Air Display' on the field, he also tells me that as he lived so close to the airfield, when he heard the sound of approaching aircraft he would run into the field to disperse the sheep. All the pilots would do a big circuit to give him time. He was sometimes rewarded by an air trip for the small price of 2/6d. He said that this was affordable to him because he had the Wenvoe newspaper round each day.

This Avro Ten was used in an attempt to force a new air service from Cardiff.

Cardiff Aeroplane Club and the Cardiff Aerodrome

Cardiff Aeroplane Club owes its foundation to a Newport man, namely, Capt. W.R. Bailey, its present Chairman. Capt. Bailey is the son of the late Mr. C.H. Bailey, who was one of the men responsible for building the great ship-repairing industry in South Wales.

Owning his own machine in 1920 he is undoubtedly the first private owner in Wales. In the intervening years he has taken nearly every flying 'course' a civilian pilot can take and today, besides being a first-class man in the air, he is an authority on the executive and administrative side of aviation. He has flown extensively on the Continent, in Kenya and Australia. *Persona grata* with everybody who is anybody in the flying world, Capt. Bailey, by his wide knowledge and influence has been largely instrumental in establishing the Cardiff Aeroplane Club so firmly in its present happy position.

Hearing in the early summer of 1931 that the Cardiff Corporation were reclaiming a part of the tide-fields of Tremorfa to make a Municipal Aerodrome and knowing from experience a great deal of the usefulness of Light Aeroplane Clubs in other parts of the country, Capt. Bailey decided that here was a fine opportunity to form such a club in Cardiff. After some preliminary negotiations with the Corporation, permission was obtained for such a club to operate from the newly made aerodrome, after which events moved rapidly.

In accordance with Air Ministry regulations for Light Airplane Clubs a Limited Company was formed in July 1931, with Capt. Bailey as Chairman, and Messrs. C.H.Keen (Deputy Chairman). G.B.Dawson, W.J.Spence-Thomas, L.Franklyn Beynon and S.Kenneth Davies as the first directors and Mr.Arthur S.Davies as secretary. The Club was called 'The Cardiff Aeroplane Club Ltd'. The directorate was considerably increased in the next few months and by September had reached twenty in number.

The establishing of an aeroplane club in a district where flying was practically unknown and which was far removed from the established flying centres demanded care, knowledge and experience. This the large board, representing as it does the professional, commercial and trade life of South Wales, was able to provide. Also, eleven members of the board had flying experience in the Flying Services during the war.

While the preliminary work of forming the club was proceeding, the work on the aerodrome went on at a pace. In the skilful hands of Mr. George Whitaker, the City Engineer, the waste and desolate tide-fields of Tremorfa were rapidly transformed into one of the finest aerodromes in the country, with the added advantage that the aerodrome itself was within ten minutes' car journey from the town centre. This is an advantage very few other large towns can claim. One of the weaknesses of many civic aerodromes is that they are too far away from the city centre to be of real use.

Ready for Action

By September 1931 the Cardiff Aerodrome was ready for use. The encircling wall was complete, the drainage working well and a good landing area levelled and cleared. A small hangar was built and pending the actual purchasing of its first aeroplane, a De Havilland Moth (G-ABEO) was hired from the De Havilland company. Flying instruction started immediately.

The first Club Instructor was Flying-Officer M.R.Edmonds, R.A.F., and the first pupil Mr. F.W.Mathias, the Glamorgan and Cardiff cricketer. Mr. Mathias has since attained the distinction of being the first Club member to qualify for his 'A' licence. In August 1931, it was thought that the successful formation of the Club should be duly celebrated, and it was decided the celebration should take the form of an Air Pageant. Saturday, October 2nd, the day chosen was dangerously near, but a later date could not be considered because of the risk of bad weather. The work entailed was enormous but somehow or other today none of the organisers quite recall how on Friday night, October 2nd, every last detail was in order.

As if in reward for their efforts, the Saturday turned out to be a perfect summer's day. The Pageant was a huge success. There is no need to recapitulate here the pageant in detail. It is still fresh in the memory of many thousands. Suffice to say a first-

Cardiff 'Splott' Aerodrome in the mid 1930s.
The photograph was taken over the River Rhymney in the East.

class programme was watched by a crowd of about 30,000 and that 56 aeroplanes were on the aerodrome during the afternoon - more planes than many South Walians thought were in existence.

Serious Setback

When Flying-Officer Edmonds resigned the post of Club Instructor, Flying-Officer Bunning was appointed in his place. For some weeks during October instruction went on merrily. New flying members joined the Club, in quite satisfactory numbers and the list of social members grew rapidly. Everything seemed 'Set Fair' for the club's future, when a serious set back was encountered. The end of October and November 1931 was a particularly wet period. It rained unceasingly for weeks. Added to this there were abnormally high tides in the Bristol Channel which nearly reached the top of the new sea wall. The strain on the new drainage was immense and it was the drainage that gave way and not the sea wall. The aerodrome flooded badly. The terrific weather conditions imperilled even this sound engineering job since it had not had time to consolidate and settle, and in December the Cardiff Aerodrome resembled the tide fields from which it had been snatched. The damage took some time to repair and it was Aril 1932 before the Air Ministry would renew the Flying Licence for the Aerodrome. The Club immediately restarted work and during the summer months a good deal of instructional flying was done, and several flying members qualified as 'A' licence pilots.

Early in the year Capt.W.R.Bailey went to Australia for an indefinite period and Mr.C.H.Keen took over the duties of Chairman during Capt. Bailey's absence. Mr. Keen took over the Club direction during a particularly critical period. As a result of the five month enforced cessation of flying, caused by the autumnal floods of 1931, interest, both individual and municipal had quite naturally fallen away. By his untiring efforts and great personal interest, Mr. Keen was largely responsible for restoring to the Club to its original enthusiasm.

During the summer of 1932 the Corporation built a fine permanent hangar on the Aerodrome which will easily accommodate twenty planes. It was decided not to hold a big pageant during 1932, but that a members 'At Home', to which pilots from other clubs should be invited, would be organised instead. This was done in October and a most successful domestic meeting was enjoyed by a large attendance of members and their guests. Thirty visiting pilots came from all parts of the country.

The Heston-Cardiff (Western Mail) Race for the Norman Nash Cup was flown and three cups put up by other directors were competed for by visiting pilots in aerobatic and landing competitions. Mr.L.R.L.Couch, a director of the Club, also gave a handsome gold pencil as the prize for a hidden treasure competition. The pencil was buried on the aerodrome. The competing planes went up and landed where they thought fit on the aerodrome - the pilot landing nearest the hidden pencil to have the prize. Unfortunately, the pencil was so well hidden that when the time came to dig it up it could not be found – and it still lies, only too successfully hidden!

This was Cardiff Aero Club's first purchase, a De Havilland Fox Moth. (Courtesy of the Western Mail)

It was September of 1932, that the Cardiff Aerodrome was fist put to a commercial use. Mr. Norman Edgar of Bristol, who owns a commercial aircraft business at the Bristol Airport, decided to start a regular Bristol-Cardiff air service. Running a De Havilland Fox Moth carrying three passengers he made the return journey twice a day. The service was most successful and was maintained with splendid regularity, only the worst weather holding up the service. Mr. Edgar to date having safely carried 800 passengers and flown 35,000 miles on this route.

The Club made another change of instructor – Mr Bunning being succeeded by Flying-Officer W.N.L.Cope. Mr. Cope was proved a most successful instructor. The September 'At Home' generated a lot of flying enthusiasm. The winter months of 1932-33 were unusually fine with lots of perfect flying weather. These facts and Flying Officer Cope's ways restarted instructional flying in earnest, and by the spring of 1933 the Club had qualified 9 'A' Class licence pilots: Messrs. F.W.Mathias; G.B.Dawson; Stanely W.J.Lewis; W.R.Brooking; J.C.Rosser; P.W.Murray-Thriepland; S.Kenneth Davies; W.T.S.Lewis and 'Jock' Thain. In addition, Flying Officer Cope had a number of other flying members flying solo and taking instruction, all of whom should qualify that year. Early in 1933 the Club was informed that the Air Ministry was prepared to grant two more clubs an Air Ministry Subsidy for qualified 'A' licensed pilots. The Club applied for one of the grants and was successful in face of great competition. No small part of the Club's success in obtaining the subsidy was due to the efforts of the then Lord Mayor of Cardiff (Ald.C.F.D. Sanders, JP), and Mr. O.Temple Morris, Member of Parliament for the Eastern Division of Cardiff. This was a great financial help to the Club as the grant was worth £25 for every 'A' licence turned out and £10 a year renewal.

Miss Pauline Gower with the Hospitals Air Pageant in 1933 at Pengam Moors.
A 1933 'Spartan' Aircraft. (Local Studies Central Library)

Making History

Early in 1933, the corporation paid the Club the great compliment of appointing them as managers of the Cardiff Aerodrome. After some preliminary meetings in the early part of the year, at which details were discussed, an agreement was drawn up between the Town Clerk of Cardiff and Mr.H.M.Ingledew, the Club's Hon. Solicitor and duly signed in April. By this agreement the Club were managers of the Cardiff Aerodrome. To facilitate the actual working, a small Management Committee was formed, to which committee members of the City Development Committee had been appointed, namely: Ald. Sir Illtyd Thomas and Counc. George Williams. The Club directors on this committee were: Capt. W.R.Bailey; Messrs. C.H. Keen; R. Cadman (the same R.Cadman on the Management Committee became Squadron Leader of 614 Squadron R.Aux. A.F.Commanding Officer 1st of June 1937 at Pengam Moors) and S.Kenneth Davies. Flying Officer Cope, the Club Instructor was appointed Aerodrome Manager.

Another great honour accorded the Club when in the same year H.R.H The Prince of Wales became the Club's Patron. This was an outstanding landmark in the history of the Cardiff Aeroplane Club and remarkable because the Prince had not given such personal recognition to any other flying organisation.

Cierva C19 Mk IV G-ABGB. Built 1931 and delivered to Alan Cobham's National Aviation Day Displays Ltd in 1932. Photographed at Cardiff Pengam Moors, June 1932.

The Pobjoy engined B.A. Swallow with Cardiff Aero Club.

Airspeed Ferry G-ABSI with Cobham's N.A.D. September 25th 1935 at Cardiff Pengam Moors.

The Cirrus engined B.A. Swallow

Cardiff Aero Club Display and Pageant - 22nd July 1933

'Over 25,000 people witnessed a three-hour spectacle at the Cardiff Aerodrome yesterday; Sir Philip Sassoon Under Secretary of State of Air opened the Show. He had flown into Cardiff in a Hawker Hart attended by three other R.A.F. Reserve machines. The London to Cardiff Air Race finished during the Pageant, all nine entrants finished the course landing within four minutes of one another. What a superb piece of handicapping!

Mr Styrian was the winner, completing the 120 miles in 52 minutes and 38 seconds. He was awarded a Western Mail prize of £20 and The Charles Keen Cup. His average speed was 136.7 miles per hour. Mr Alex Henshaw was second and won £5 and The Wellsteed Cup in 57minutes and 45 seconds.

The star 'Crasher' of Hollywood 'Wing' Wyndham repeated some of his film exploits. Capt. Unwins of Bristol, who holds the World's height record (43,976 feet) gave a remarkable exhibition of high speed diving, power and manoeuvrability in his 'Bristol Bulldog'. Then we saw the discipline of '501' Bombing Squadron, under Squadron Leader W.Elliott D.F.C., give a display.

Mr.C.B.Field of London gave a display of 'Crazy Flying', but the most thrilling event was the delayed parachute jump from 3,000 feet by the one armed expert Wyndham (Wingy). He did not open his parachute until he was 500 feet from the ground.

Hundreds of people took to the air on the joy-rides until late in to the day. There were many important people who were impressed and this, a comment from a

CARDIFF AIRPORT
PENGAM   SPLOTT
Wednesday & Thursday, June I & 2

CONTINUOUS
PROGRAMME OF
THRILLS

Startling Acrobatic Feats.
Wonderful Upside-down Flying.
Aeroplane-towed Gliding.   ::
Radio-controlled Flying.   ::
Daring   Parachute   Descents.
Exciting Pylon Race.   ::   ::
Grand Fly-past in Formation.
Stunting in Formation.   ::   ::
" How Not to Fly."   ::   ::
Aerial Marksmanship. ::   ::
The   world-famous   " Golden
   Arrow " Racing Car.
FLIGHTS FROM 4/-.

THE BIG EVENT OF CIVIC WEEK
I2 AIRCRAFT   ::   20 EVENTS
under the personal direction of Sir Alan Cobham.
Admission : 1/3 *; Children, 6d. ; Motor Cars, 1/-.*
11.30 a.m. till dusk. Special Evening Display, 6.0 p.m.

94/95 Advertisements from Official Handbook and Programme, City of Cardiff Civic Week, 2-11 June, 1932

Swansea councillor "One cannot be but impressed with the tremendous importance of work that has been done at Cardiff Airport and we must do the same at Swansea."' (Article courtesy of Cardiff Central Library).

The Club closed at Pengam and moved to Rhoose in 1954.

The club flourished quite well during the years up to the outbreak of war with a good membership, a clubhouse and hangar. Then in 1936 The Air Ministry began their surveys into the possibility of making Pengam Moors in to R.A.F. Cardiff.

By 1937 it was settled that Cardiff would be a base for 614 County of Glamorgan Auxiliary Air Force Squadron. With Army Cooperation Command, the building of hangars and other buildings began. Richard Cadman, the Aero Club's Chairman became Squadron Leader Cadman O.C. of 614 Squad.

The airfield was shared by Western Airways, Cardiff Aero Club and the Royal Air Force. Cardiff Aero was to act as managers of the base until the outbreak of war. In those last months of peace the club had approximately eight aircraft on charge: three Gypsy Moths, two B.A. Swallows (one engined with a Pobjoy and one with an ADC Cirrus engine), a Hornet Moth and two Tiger Moths. The club also had a 'Wicko', a

DH Fox Moth.

cabin for two seats and high wing monoplane. With these aircraft the club ran down on the advent of the Second World War.

At the end of the War the club resumed its activities, but without the same volume and interest. They had accidents as all clubs do, such as in September 1951 when the pilot of a Tiger Moth and the pilot of an Auster Autocrat both from Cardiff, did what was described as 'dog-fighting' over Dinas Powis (five miles from Pengam). They collided with each other and fell from the sky to crash on Dinas Common. Both men were killed. Mr. Doug Kemp, the Chief Instructor and Dennis Panes, who was in charge of maintenance.

Cardiff Aero Club had a Hornet Moth similar to the above with the registration G-ADMT.

Cardiff Aero Club Post War Tiger Moth G-ANEV.

At this time, in the fifties, the club was flying Hornet Moth G-ADMT, three Tiger Moths and two Auster Autocrats. Then in 1958 Tiger Moth AG-ANEV, taking off into an easterly wind and heading, struggled and then stalled finally crashing on St Mellons golf course, causing the deaths of Mr Moss Eddems an experienced pilot and a pupil (name not known). The club carried on flying from Pengam long after the airlines and

Wicko Aircraft at Cardiff Aero Club Pengam Moors (Central Library).

R.A.F. had gone on 1st April 1954. The club faded away rather than died about 1957 never to reappear.

The Cardiff Ultra Light Club

This club had a brief history jammed between the end of the War and airfields closure. The club had a 'Tipsy' light monoplane which was fitted with a 50 HP

35

A Tiger Moth (G-AHVU) outside the hangar at Pengam. (Courtesy of M. Amundsen)

Cardiff Aero Club - A post War Auster 'Autocrat' (G-AHSW) at Pengam. (Courtesy of M. Amundsen)

'Tipsy' of Cardiff Ultra Light Aero Club (Post War). (Courtesy of M. Amundsen)

Walter Micron engine. It seems that this aircraft caused the death of a pilot. On taking off into an easterly heading the 'Tipsy' stalled and went down killing Mr Preece the pilot.

A Brief History of Western Airways

In 1931 Norman Edgar operated an air taxi service along with others called Bristol Air Taxis. The company that was later named Western Airways had begun as Norman Edgar Airways and on September 26th 1932 he began a twice daily service from Bristol to Cardiff with a DH 'Fox Moth' G-ABYO, carrying three passengers. This was the same

The Spider Fokker (G-EBTS) at Whitchurch Bristol.

service that failed when operated by British Air Navigation only two months previously. Their failure was to do with the uneconomic Fokker F VII G-EBTS 'Spider' which had eight seats to fill but they were never busy enough to fill all eight places.

Norman Edgar slowly built up his clientele. The river Severn estuary always made the South Wales and South West journey difficult by road or rail and business men could save much time by flying, and even holiday makers with money to spare could see the advantages of a trip over the water by aeroplane. Both Whitchurch (Bristol) and Splott (Cardiff) as it was called then were close to the town centres and access to

Western Airways D.H. Dragons lined up at Cardiff Airport (Ted Williams).

shops and further journeys by train. Edgar ordered a DH 84 Dragon for the route.

The company became 'Western Airways' and Lord Apsley became chairman with Norman Edgar as managing Director a week after delivery of the DH 84 Dragon. The company opened a Bristol to Le Touquet (Paris) route on May 23rd 1935. To cope with this extra work a DH 84 Dragon was leased from Jersey Airways but it was written off near Cardiff on July 23rd 1935.

The newly built airport at Weston-Super-Mare began services at the end of May 1936 and the first Western Airways aircraft to use Weston was a DH 84 Dragon G-ACJT which landed on 4th of June 1936. The Air Ministry did not actually grant a licence for Weston until 25th June, before which 1,700 passengers had already made flights to Weston from Cardiff. It was at this time, January 1938 that the company

Kings Flight DH89 sold to Norman Edgar of Western Airways.

was taken over by the Straight Corporation and continued to grow. The company's maintenance had always been done by Portsmouth, Southsea and Isle of Wight Aviation but now had their own engineering base at Weston.

Cambrian Air Services who had loose links with Western had aspirations to join in this fruitful route to Weston and Bristol based at Cardiff, but was rebuffed again and

G-ACTU Western Airways leaving Weston for Cardiff. Two engined Dragon-Rapide.

again. Much of the success of this Cardiff to Weston route was due to Welsh miners taking their days off in Weston and on Sunday evening the whole fleet were drawn up for the last flight back to Cardiff.

Western Airways now had a fleet of DH 84 Dragons and DH 89 Dragon Rapides and were all repainted Straight Corporation colours, metallic blue-grey with lettering, crim-

G-AETM 4 engine Western Airways D.H. 86B Express sold to Finland December 1939.

son with white edging. The rudders were striped with 11 red and 10 white bands. At this time, on the takeover by Straights, some 40,000 passengers had flown the ten-minute Cardiff trip at a fare of nine shillings and sixpence return. It was preferable to three hours by train or one hour by Campbell steamer. One of the Rapides was G-ADDD, the first aircraft used by the Kings Flight on its formation in July 1936. It was previously privately owned by HRH Prince Edward, Prince of Wales and purchased by Norman Edgar for £3,345 on May 8th 1937. During 1938 Western had flown a Friday to Monday Birmingham to Weston service for people to have a weekend break by the sea in 45 minutes' travel time. There were services to Manchester offering pleasure flying from Manchester airport and a lot of charter work was also done.

The Air Navigation Act of 1936 demanded that as from 1st November 1938 it would be an offence to fly a passenger service without a licence from the Air Transport Authority. Western Airways made applications for route licences which were granted following a public hearing. These licences allowed operators exclusive rights on these routes. There were protests from Railway Air Services who competed on most of the routes applied for.

Provisional licences were granted to Western in October for the routes between Cardiff and Weston and Weston to Swansea. Western started a night service schedule between Weston and Cardiff on October 2nd 1938, these flights were the first internal night scheduled flights within the UK. The first night flight was with DH 89 G-ADDD. The BBC arranged for the take-off from Weston and the landing at Cardiff along with the comments on board during the flight to be broadcast live.

In April 1939 DH 86b G-AETM was purchased from Allied Airways to cope with the expected increase in passengers on the Cardiff to Weston route in the summer months, and the company obtained a fixed term lease of 42 years. At Weston-Super-Mare Airport plans were drawn up for the new buildings required, such as terminals, hangars and the Flying Training School that Western Airways were to operate.

On May 8th 1939 Western started a Manchester to Penzance service calling at Barnstaple and on the same day a twice-daily Swansea-Barnstaple-Newquay (Trebelzue) to Penzance (St. Just) service operated with DH 84's. 1939 also saw the start of a thrice-daily Manchester-Birmingham-Bristol-Weston service.

Demand for air travel was now at such a rate that over the five days of Whitsun 2,555 passengers were carried from Weston, allowing the claim to a world record.

With the outbreak of World War Two the company were chartered early on for Army Cooperation flights and then the company was contracted to provide the facilities for a navigation school. A new hangar of 60,000 square feet was erected and the runway area was extended. On September 5th 1939 the number 5 Civil Air Navigation School was formed at Weston. Commanded by W.R.Cummings who had been director of training at the Straight Corporation. The school operated Avro Ansons giving Western a valuable insight into this aircraft for later years.

The company with its extensive maintenance facility became a contractor for the Ministry of Aircraft Production and all of the company's fleet of Dragons and Rapides were commanded into the RAF during 1940. The airfield was taken over by the RAF on 1st May 1940 and a factory was opened for the production of Bristol Beaufighters on the South West boundary. An assembly factory was built to the North of the airfield.

No.10 Elementary Flying Training School arrived from Yatesbury on September 7th 1940 and No. 5 A.O.N.S. (navigation school) was transferred to South Africa on August 22nd 1940. During the War the company repaired Avro Ansons under the Civilian Repair Organisation. It was 1946 when the airfield was handed over to the Ministry of Civil Aviation following the War.

Commercial flying was resumed and during August Western purchased the first of the civilianised Avro Ansons, known as Avro 19's from surplus RAF Stoke for use in flying training and charter work, they entered service in September 1946. May 1948 saw the Ansons operating a scheduled passenger service between Western and Pengam Moors through an associate agreement with British European Airways. This came about because of the nationalisation in 1946 of the nation's internal airlines, but the route was to be reopened and flown in association with Cambrian Air Services. The first flight was on May 25th 1948 and the day after the service resumed 98 passengers travelled from Weston to Cardiff and 94 from Cardiff to Weston.

Western Airways were operating the Ansons but Cambrian operated their DH 89's G-AGZJ, G-AKUB and G-AKUC; both companies were busy. During 1948 six services a day were flown in each direction, but July and for the rest of the summer these were increased to thirteen each way. The original agreement for the operation of the route was to run until October 11th 1948, but after negotiations with BEA they were granted a twelve-month extension.

The Cardiff to Weston service was operated by Western until the summer of 1949 when difficulties in operating jointly with Cambrian Air Services and the removal of Cardiff Airport from Pengam Moors to Rhoose made the route uneconomic for Western Airways, so Cambrian took over the whole operation.

The Ansons of Western took up charter work and they charged ten pence a customer to handle Cambrian's passengers at Weston. The large scale of charter flights continued until 1952 when the last Anson was sold. Western Airways concentrated all their efforts on its repair, overhaul and maintenance of aircraft at Weston-Super-Mare airport. Sub-contract work was undertaken for Westlands Wyvern long-range naval fighter, flaps and wing tanks were made for the DH Vampire and from the 1950's onwards the company built airframe components for the Bristol 170 Freighter. This began with the manufacture of control surfaces, ailerons, elevators rudders, flaps tailplanes and doors.

The Western Company also became sub-contractor to work on the Bristol Britannia Airliner, the Concorde and other aircraft; they also did work for Rolls Royce on the RB2-11 engine. The last contract was completed in 1980. Airport licences lapsed in 1978 when Western relinquished their operating licence, thus ending all flying activities of Western Airways Ltd.

The next airline to begin operations here was the G.W.R. who started an air service from Cardiff to Plymouth via Haldon on 12th April 1933 after trials the previous day. They operated twice daily in each direction on weekdays until 22nd May. The route was then extended to Birmingham (Castle Bromwich) and the frequency was cut to once a day on weekdays until the route was closed for the winter on 30th

Westland Wessex at Cardiff Airport.

A Westland Wessex (G-AAGW) departs from Cardiff (Pengam) on its inaugural flight. 11th April 1933. Great Western Railway Service. A Wessex (G-EBXK) is on the ground.

September. This route's attempt to make money failed but it was a success for the customers: 50 minutes to Haldon at a cost of £3 and 75 minutes to Plymouth at a cost of £3.10. G.W.R. used the Westland Wessex.

All the railway companies including Southern, G.W.R., L.M.S. and L.N.E.R. had realised that they must amalgamate their airlines to make profits, and this resulted in the formation of Railway Air Services. With this new company, the route Cardiff-Haldon-Plymouth and later Birmingham and Liverpool Speke were re-introduced. On 7th May 1934 there were flights once a day in each direction on weekdays. These routes were uneconomical and the trip became Cardiff-Weston-Bristol on 25th May

'City of Cardiff' at Cardiff Airport (Pengam). D.H. Dragon Railway Air Services.

1936 and the Cardiff-Weston service became hourly. These routes continued much the same until the War, and the Rail Air Services returned post-war. On 31st July 1946 the routes from Cardiff to Bristol and Cardiff to Weston were re-established. The Bristol route was flown six times every weekday and the Weston route no less than fourteen times in each direction daily.

Railways Air Services ceased all operations 31st January 1947. The next, and by far the largest and most important airline to commence operations at Pengam was Cambrian Air services. The initial impetus for the formation of this famous company came from the passion for flying and patriotism of a man named S. Kenneth Davis. He was a class 'A' licence holder by 1932 and he flew as much as possible. He brought £750 plus an old 'Gypsy Moth' to form an airline.

In May 1935 the three directors Mr Davis, Mr G.H. Fox and Colonel R. G. Llewellyn held a meeting and decided to establish a regional office at Pengam Moors, Cardiff.

The company carried passengers in the Moth and looked for ways to expand. They asked Western Airways if they could join them but they were rebuffed. When all civil

flying ceased at the outbreak of the Second World War, Cambrian took over part of a hangar and set up an engineering unit making parts for parachutes etc.

While the civil airlines were going on with their peaceful work, and the Cardiff aero club prospered, the rumblings of re-armament were heard at the Air Ministry. Sites were being looked at all over the UK and Pengam Moors was to be one of them. The following words are from the Western Mail & Echo detailing the planning that was to enhance this comparatively new and small Aerodrome.

'An official of the Air Ministry surveyed the Cardiff Aerodrome on Tuesday in connection with the establishment in Wales preferably near a large town to enable easy attendance of the civilian members of a new territorial type organisation that would attract and train young men.

It was to be an Auxiliary Air Force Squadron. The merits of Cardiff Airport were discussed when the Air Ministry Surveyor Mr Meyrick James met Sir Illtyd Thomas

(Chairman of the Airport Committee), Mr S.K. Davies, Capt. Freddie Mathias, Mr Richard Cadman of Cardiff Aeroplane Club and the City Engineer Mr Geo Whitaker. Nothing definite had been decided about the location of the squadron except that it would be somewhere in Wales.

Four new squadrons were to be formed, one in Scotland, one in Wales and two in England. They were to be a new type, formed with the intention of co-operating with the Territorial Army. The personnel of the squadrons would be almost entirely non-regular and would be recruited from the immediately vicinity, about 18 officers and nearly four times as many other ranks. Other sites would be inspected in due course.'

22nd August 1936
Mr Meyrick James had surveyed several other sites including St Athan as possible locations.

2nd September 1936
The Air Ministry has asked the Cardiff Corporation to extend Cardiff Airport. It was understood that the Air Ministry had informed the Corporation that the greatest possible area must be provided for the aerodrome and one of the suggestions was that some of the allotments adjoining the airport would be taken over for that purpose. The Air Ministry had also asked for the possibility of filling up the cut near the Rhymney River. The City Engineer had been asked to submit a report on this proposal. (Western Mail & Echo).

Western Mail & Echo October 1936
Auxiliary Squadron for Glamorgan Headquarters at Splott
'As with all Squadrons Adjutant, Assistant Adj. and stores officers were to be regular R.A.F. personnel. There would be approximately 40 other regular ranks. The C.O. would be an Auxiliary Officer; recruits would be taken on a four-year engagement.'

Western Mail 19th November 1936
'Four Air Ministry officials representing the Ministry proper, R.A.F. and civil aviation interests, visited Cardiff Airport to review arrangements for the expansion of the airport and accommodation of the Aux. Air Force.'

Western Mail January 1937
'Some 700-800 Cardiff allotment holders will be forced to give up their plots by the end of September to make way for developments of Pengam for the Aux. Air Force. The position of existing civil airways hangar would be changed and a barracks and stores constructed.'

Western Mail 27th January 1937
'Air Ministry state that they intend to form the squadron at Cardiff. They also notify

the corporation that the allotments on the north and west sides would be required. The buildings would be at the northeast corner. Cardiff Aero Club to move to northwest corner, as it will be when the allotments are included. The entrance to the civil part of the aerodrome being in Tweedsmuir Road.'

Western Mail 3rd February 1937
Air factory for Cardiff.
'A semi-private company was negotiating to buy 10 acres of land from the Corporation to build a factory (Machine Products Ltd) at Pengam. The fields at the time were football pitches.'

Western Mail 24th February 1937
'The Air Ministry has arranged to buy nine acres at Pengam Farm for the manufacture of aircraft parts. The price is 565 pounds per acre.'

Western Mail 23rd April 1937
Recruiting for the Aux. Squadron to commence on 1st June.
'The Air Ministry proposals for the future of Cardiff Aerodrome were discussed by the Corporation Airport Committee on Friday 25th, when it was decided to recommend the acceptance of the plans put forward, subject to minor adjustments.

'The hangars, offices and barracks equipment will be placed on each side of Whitaker Road and on part of the aerodrome adjoining. Temporarily the existing hangar and clubhouse will remain where they stand, but it may be necessary to remove the Western Airways offices for a short period to the south west of the existing hangar. Eventually it is intended to remove the hangar, clubhouse and offices to the southwest corner of the aerodrome.'

Western Mail 22nd May 1937
'A Royal Air Force auxiliary unit is due to arrive at Cardiff Airport on June 1st. It is expected to comprise several officers who will give instructions, and a number of N.C.O.'s and men to service the machines, which will probably be AVRO trainers.'

(Courtesy of Cardiff Central Library and Ted Chamberlain)

1939 - 1945

614 Squadron (County of Glamorgan) R.Aux. A.F.

A survey by The Air Ministry on Tuesday 19th August 1936 at Splott airport resulted in the purchase of allotments on the edge on the field, and a decision to go ahead with the building of an R.Aux. A.F. station. There was to be an allocation of regular officers and a nucleus of sixty regular other ranks, but in the event only eleven O/Rs arrived. Orders were issued for the hangars and other buildings between September 1936 and 1938; the construction was urgent and rapid.

Hangars are being erected behind this Hawker Hector at Pengam Moors. A pilot inspects the tail plane whilst the Napier Dagger engine is running.

It was formed as the only Auxiliary Squadron in Wales on 1st June 1937 at Pengam Moors, Cardiff. It was designated an Army co-operation role in No. 22 group. Squadron Leader Cadman was C.O. and Flying Officer M.G.F. Pedley the Adjutant. Before a full squadron complement could be trained, the war started with seven pilots on a course of Army co-op training at Old Sarum Wiltshire.

The Squadron, by 3rd September 1939 was equipped with Hawker Hectors, Hinds

Three 614 Sq. 'Hectors' fly over Cardiff's Civic Centre. 1938.

and an Avro Tutor for initial flying training. On 18th September Squadron Leader Cadman was posted to become Station Commander at R.A.F. Cardiff (Pengam Moors). L.J. Stickely R.A.F. became The Squadron C.O. with Flying Officer R.E.C. Cadman as Adjutant.

On 2nd October the Squadron moved to R.A.F. Odiham Hampshire and on 10th

614 Squadron Section over the Vale of Glamorgan. 1938 'Hawker Hectors'.

614 Squadron R. Aux.A.F. The initial squadron pilots in front of their Hawker 'Hectors'. (1937).

October a new Squadron was formed from 'B' Flight of 614, known for a few days as 614 'A' Squadron, but then became No.225 Squadron R.A.F. By this time 614 was flying Lysanders Mk II.

On 8th November 1939, Squadron Leader W. R. Wills-Sandford was appointed to command and the 614 Squadron handed over most of their Hinds and Lysander aircraft to the last formed Aux. A.F. Squadron The City of Manchester No. 613, which was also at Odiham.

Lysander of 614A Squadron.

Intensive training took place to bring the crews up to operational standard, and then the bisecting of 614 Squadron continued, with crews who were deemed ready leaving the Squadron to join the Air Component in France for liaison work with the Expeditionary Force.

In May 1940, with the German Army pushing into the low countries, six aircraft were deployed to Amiens-Glisy airfield to act as spotters for British and French artillery. This all ended at the embarkation at Dunkirk. The Squadron was then ordered to Grange Mouth near Edinburgh with detachments to Evanton, Montrose, Longman, Dumfries and Tangmere for Army co-op and convoy patrols to release Hurricanes and Spitfires to go south to carry out tactical reconnaissance exercise and 'A' Flight maintained shipping cover from Montrose down as far as Berwick-on-Tweed.

Once the Battle of Britain was won, the opportunity was taken on 25th September 1940 to form another Squadron on a nucleus of 614 personnel plus 'A' Flight of No.4 Squadron, and No.241 Squadron began to form at Inverness. 241 and the previous birth of 225 Squadrons were to later become magnificent Photo-Reconnaissance Squadrons. Then a detachment of Lysanders of 614 was sent to Tangmere for air-sea rescue work. Then on 9th October, the Squadron received the Lysander III and when volunteers were sought after for Bolton-Paul, Defiant night fighters, they left to form yet another Squadron. In April 1941 the Squadron had detachments at Macmerry, Inverness, Elgin and Westhampnett, but were delighted to learn it had done its share of forming other units, and was now entitled to take a part in the growing offensive.

The Bristol Blenheim Mark IV Light Bomber was allocated to 614 and under Wing Commander Skelton and Squadron Leader B.R. Macnamara, conversion to the type was so rapid that some crews flew down to West Raynham Norfolk during May 1941 to operate 'intruder' missions against German airfields. In support of The First Thousand Plan on 30/31st May, 614's Blenheim's attacked Bonn airfield to prevent

614 County of Glamorgan equipped with Blenheim Vs embarked for North Africa to back up the Army in Tunisia where they suffered severe losses.

The last vestiges of R.A.F. occupation. Sgts Mess, Pengam Moors, St. Albans Club.

night fighters taking off to interfere with the main force. By July under Wing Commander Sutton there were twenty-two trained crews on strength (the highest ever) and there were big moves ahead. The Mark V Bisley was to be their equipment and North Africa the destination. From Odiham the Squadron flew to Portraeth, Cornwall and in November set off for Gibraltar (one failed to arrive). By 18th November, the Squadron was part of No. 326 wing at Blida in Algeria, commanded by Group Captain Laurence Sinclair G.C., C.B.E., D.S.O. and B.A.R., a distinguished Blenheim pilot.

Pengam Moors Officers Mess and Quarters.

The Squadron went on to achieve fame in North Africa though they received heavy losses. On one occasion ten aircraft set out without escort and successfully bombed their target from 200 feet, only to meet sixty M.E. 109's who bounced them and shot all ten down.

The Squadron went on to further fame in Italy, where they were re-equipped with Halifax 11s at Celone under Wing Commander Russell, and became a heavy bomber unit. Targets at Genoa, Sofia in Bulgaria and acting as target marking force for 205 Group, bombing Ploesti, and Iron Gates canal (Romania's key waterway), and as part of a joint U.S.AAF & R.A.F. Group, struck targets in Yugoslavia, Greece, Bulgaria, Italy and Hungary. Then came visits to Munich. At the end of the War in Europe, the Squadron flew prisoners of war home to the U.K., 25 in each Liberator. In July 1945 came the order to disband, and No. 214 Squadron R.A.F. took over the Liberators.

On 26th August 1947, the Squadron reformed at Llandow in The Auxiliary Airforce with Spitfire 16's first then Spitfire 22's a few months later. The first peacetime C.O. was Squadron Leader W.H. Irving D.F.C. In July 1950 the Squadron re-equipped with D.H.Vampires and Squadron Leader E.H. Mc Hardy D.S.O., D.F.C. and B.A.R., Croix-De-Guerre took command. In 1954 the Fighter-Bomber MK5 was being flown with a few F.B. 9's later. Then the blow came when all R.Aux. A.F. Squadrons were told to disband. 614 has to this day a lively and active association. The club has an outstanding magazine and they enjoy reunions and trips to bases in the U.K. The editor and driving force is Mr David Park of 5 Saffron Drive, St Mellons, Cardiff.

Military use of Pengam Moors R.A.F Cardiff 1937 - 1945

6 14 Squadron, up to its mobilisation and posting off Odiham in October 1939, had Cardiff as its H.Q. The weekend training and evening classes for ground and aircrew began to mould the group into shape. Then in October 1939 they left, never to return. This didn't mean the airfield became deserted, as different support units made their home at Pengam. Added to the arrivals and departures of aircraft for J.Currans, Air Dispatch Co. and the aircraft flown in for 52M.U. (some came by road), the field was kept fairly busy.

The aircraft carrier 'Courageous' was torpedoed and sunk by a U-boat on Sunday 17th September 1939, just a fortnight after the war started. The survivors of 815 Squadron were reformed at Worthy Down airfield in Hampshire, but their next operations were to be over the Bristol Channel.

The squadron, with their Fairy 'Swordfish' aircraft flew to Cardiff Pengam Moors in January 1940 where they were to develop flying anti-submarine patrols usually at dawn to Lundy island and back, to keep submarines from surfacing. The loss of allied shipping in the area was great in 1940. The squadron was troubled by the wet conditions at Pengam and were unable to take off and land safely, so many patrols were missed. No.815 squadron left Cardiff after only a few months on posting to Bircham Newton.

615 Squadron F.A.A. patrol the Bristol Channel from Pengam Moors. January 1940.

While at Cardiff, and owing to the sinking of 'Courageous', the aircrews were feted and a Lord Mayor's reception at the City Hall in February 1940 was held. No.8 A.A.C.U. (Anti-Aircraft Co-operation Unit), arrived in November 1940 from Weston Zoyland to help the 9th Anti-Aircraft division in the area of South Wales in training, and practice shoots. This unit had been formed just five months before at Ringway Airport, had they been sent briefly to Weston Zoyland in Somerset and then on to Pengam Moors. Here they stayed for over three years until they disbanded on 8th December 1943. They came equipped at various times with all sorts of obscure aircraft because of the shortage of serviceable modern types. Initially there were D.H. Dragons, Dragon Rapides, Dragonfly and then the three types of General Aircraft Co, Monospars, the S6, S12 and S25; also, Blenheims, Lysanders, Dominies and later Oxfords and Masters were employed.

Officers of 615 Fleet Air Arm Squadron with the Lord Mayor at Cardiff's City Hall. (C. Ashworth)

Monospar St.25 (8 AACU) Pengam. No. 8 Anti-Aircraft Co-Op Unit.

D.H. Dominie. 8 AACU (Anti-Aircraft Co-operation Unit), Pengam Moors.

Monospar ST 12. 8 AACU, Pengam Moors.

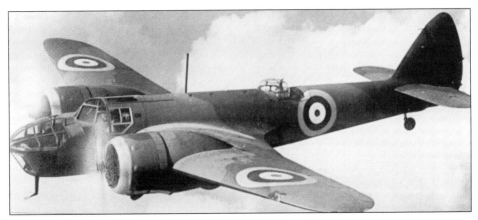

Blenheim MK IV. 8 AACU, Pengam Moors.

With the approach of D. Day, vast quantities of U.S.A.F. and Army supplies were held here. The Americans had stores ready for the Continent and their C47's landed at Pengam to pick up these stores as, and when they were needed in France. They assembled and tested a Squadron of Piper Cubs here; around a dozen of these A.O.P. aircraft were handled. They had been shipped in crates from then U.S.A. to Cardiff Docks, and brought by road to the airfield sheds of John Currans where the American army engineers assembled them. The majority of these Cubs were then flown off to the Glider Field in Llanishen, and the strip at Heath Camp.

Air Dispatch Company fulfilled a lot of work outside the M.A.P. contracts. Their apron was swamped with odd jobs including Beechcraft, DC47, Vengeance, Thunderbolt, Avenger and even a Marauder landing on a 960 yd x 50 yd runway.

587 Squadron sent a detachment to Pengam from 10th April 1944 to 1st October 1944 with their Martinets, Henleys and Hurricane IIC's. This unit had been formed

Miles Master MKIII. 587 Squadron. Pengam.

Hawker 'Henley' Target Tug. 587 Squadron, Pengam.

Hurricane IIc, 587 Squadron, Pengam Moors.

at Weston Zoyland on 1st December 1943 and the aircraft were coded M4, and this squadron was the result of the merging of three separate Flights – 1600 and 1601 Target – towing flights and No.1625 Anti-Aircraft Co-op Flight. The squadron was equipped with Oxfords, Masters, Vengeance, Henley and Hurricane IIC. These aircraft were all providing target practice for anti-aircraft batteries and sometimes Air-to-Air Gunnery training.

286 Squadron had a detachment to Pengam at various periods between April 1942 and May 1945. Formed from No.10 group anti-aircraft co-op training at Filton on 17th November 1941, it was simply renamed No.286 Squadron with Oxfords, Defiants and Masters, Martinet and Lysander. The unit code was NW and was disbanded 16th May 1945 at Weston Zoyland.

Auster V. 663 Squadron, Pengam Moors. These were Air Observation Posts used by the Army for spotting shell fire fall.

663 Squadron 1952 flight from Llandow arrived on 15th October 1949 with A.O.P. Auster V's until 18th June 1953, when they returned to Llandow as Pengam's flying days were coming to an end.

At the end of the War the Ministry of Defence opened Reserve Flying Schools around the country to maintain the flying skills among the released aircrews, and to teach new pupils. One of these schools was established at Pengam Moors, Cardiff. Mr Ted Williams joined from the R.A.F. and became Equipment Safety Officer responsible for parachutes etc. Wing Commander Kinnear was C.O. of 3 R.F.S., who was also at the time manager of the adjacent Cambrian Airways. In charge of flying was Squadron Leader Dalrymple. Instructors were Flight Sgt. Hembry and Sgt. Theophilus.

3 reserve Flying School at Pengam Moors. 'Chipmunk' Pilot Trainer. The lad is Maxwell Morris. (Ted Williams)

On charge were 3 Tiger Moths No's: NL 929, T5968 and T6095 and 5 Chipmunks. There were two Oxfords and two Ansons for navigation and wireless training. Mr Ted Williams was there until closure in 1953 and remembers the flying off of the unit's last aircraft, two Tiger Moths.

While there, Ted learned a lot about aircraft repair and maintenance and made himself pretty indispensable, as he was one of the few people still conversant with fabric and doping on the airfield. He did much work for 3 R.F.S. and Cambrian Airways five Dragon Rapides No's: G-AKUB, G-AKLU, G-AKCL, G-AKAT and G-AKSI, AFSK. The Cambrian staff there were: Chief Engineer Laurie Moore, Maintenance Ken Peat and engineers: Percy Smith, David Sawyer and Doug Summers, Squadron Leader Dalrymple, Flight Sgt. Hembry, and Sgt. Theophilus (instructors).

Airspeed Oxford with No. 3 Reserve flying School. Pengam Moors.
Used for navigation and wireless training.

Here is Mr Goff Watkins' story of his later war flying with the R.A.F. and No.3 Reserve Flying School.

'In 1944, like so many other Air Training Corps Cadets, I enlisted at Penarth for aircrew service in the R.A.F. Aged 17 I eagerly awaited call up. The following August I was summoned to R.A.F. Cosford for two days' aptitude tests.

'Fortunately I passed and at the final interview I was told that only 4% of those whom had been previously selected would now await R.A.F. call up. Three months later I received yet another letter requiring me to attend at the Grand Hotel Torquay for a further four days of aptitude tests. At this stage of the War the R.A.F. had a surplus of aircrew, and this time I knew my number was up. Some three weeks later I was informed by letter that my services were no longer required by the R.A.F. I immediately applied to join the Fleet Air Arm, went for medical and aptitude test, which I passed and was then informed that I could not be attested until I had received my discharge papers from the R.A.F. I wrote to the Air Ministry requesting these papers and

A R.A.F. Trainer Tiger Moth. A beautiful example newly overhauled and painted.

they were good enough to send them to me two days after my calling up papers for the Army. These required me to report to the Primary Training Centre at Fort George, some twelve miles from Inverness. The whole intake (approx 2,000 recruits) was composed of ex R.A.F. aircrew awaiting call up. At the first available opportunity I volunteered for the Glider Pilot Regiment along with eight of my comrades. The selection board was at Doncaster Racecourse, which was a staging camp. The second and third nights were spent at N.A.A.F.I. Club. Mid July 1945 found us at Fargo Camp Salisbury. There were six weeks of further square bashing, schemes, assault courses and then Elementary Flying Training School. At this time the Regiment used four E.F.T.A.'s - Booker, (High Wycombe), Panshanger, near Hereford, Yatesbury and Marshals of Cambridge, which was the one I was sent to. This was a three-month course, identical to that of the R.A.F. pilot trainee, the only difference being, we did not study engines. The ground subjects were Navigation, Airmanship, Meteorology, Principles of Flight, Interpretation of air Photographs and Aircraft recognition.

'Our course was split into two, alternating between ground subjects morning and flying in the afternoon. On leaving Cambridge, my next station was Croughton in the Midlands, where I did ten hours on Hotspur gliders before being posted to Elsham Wolds in Lincolnshire, where I met up with my first pilot. Some five months later it was decreed that the G.P.R. would be reduced to two squadrons, each having sixty crews (120 pilots). I was signed on the 'b' scheme for three years regular army service. In November 1946 I commenced my training for first pilot, and did yet again and another full EFTS, again on Tiger Moths at Booker. Thence to Wellesbourne Mountford where I did thirty-five hours on Hotspurs. From Wellesbourne to North Luffenham in Rutland, where I did fifteen hours on Horsa gliders, and was presented with the Army Flying Badge (1st Pilot) on 4th December 1947. I did a stint at Oakington, and Waterbeach, and when the Berlin Airlift started I went on several refresher courses on Tiger Moths. All the Dakotas were required in Germany. In early 1949 the powers that be decided to employ glider pilots as second pilots on the new H.P. 'Hastings' aircraft, and I was one of the first twelve to be selected. About a week before we were to leave for Germany, word came through that our orderly room Sergeant had passed his War Office Selection Board for training as an officer. One morning just after a flight in the Tiger Moth, I was approached by our C.O. who asked me if I would do the job of Orderly Room Sergeant until he could find a suitable replacement. Before joining up I had worked in a solicitor's office, and for two years had been a Magistrates Clerk's Assistant at Abergavenny. I pointed out to him that I was due to go to Germany the following week, and he told me that when further replacements were needed I could go then. My replacement was a Sgt. Joe Toal (for Germany) who was killed with the other members of his crew when a Hasting crashed taking off at Tegel in July 1949. I never did get to Germany, and a suitable replacement Orderly Room Sgt. Was found three weeks before I was demobbed.

'In February 1950 I commenced training at the Government Training Centre Leicester as a trainee mechanical engineering Draughtsman, and whilst there joined No.7 Reserve Flying School at Desford, and given the rank of Pilot 4. For about two or three years the R.A.F. had dispensed with the ranks of Sgt., Flight Sgt., and Warrant Officer, and substituted (for Pilots, the ranks of Pilot 4, Pilot 3, Pilot 2, Pilot 1, and Master Pilot) Pilot 2 was the equivalent of Flight Sgt. and his insignia was three stars in a wreath of Laurel leaves. On receiving his wings the pilot was given the rank of P4. On completion of my draughtsman's course I was fortunate to obtain a position with Rhymney Engineering Cardiff, and so transferred to No.3 Reserve Flying School at Pengam Moors. After introducing myself to the C.O. Wing Commander Kinnear, who was also the manager of Cambrian Airways there at the time. He told me that they could not operated Tiger Moths for long periods in the winter months, because of airfield flooding. Pengam Moors had a single runway, and as the Tiger Moth was fitted with a tail skid, they could not use the runway.

'This was the reason why I decided to write to the C.O. of No.614 A.A.F. squadron at Llandow. I went for an interview with log books, and was told I could join, but until confirmation from Fighter Command had been received it would be at my own expense. I was with them for about three months, and was then told that I could not join as I had not completed a Service Flying Training School course. I used to act as safety pilot when the boys wanted to practice instrument flying in the 'Meteor 7'. Whilst with 614 Squadron I did 2½ hours duel on the 'Harvard' and a ½ hr duel on the 'Meteor'.

'I was very sad at leaving 614 Squadron and went back to 3R.F.S. at Pengam. I did 33 hours on Tiger Moths between May and August 1951. In September 1951 I was able to find employment in Abergavenny (my home town) and did no further flying at Pengam Moors. In 1953 the R.A.F.V.R. Flying Schools were disbanded.' Goff Watkins

This was the last flying unit of the R.A.F. at Pengam Moors.

On the outbreak of war plans were implemented to put civilians of the UK into useful war production. At Pengam it took the form of the companies of Air

No. 3 Reserve Flying School at Pengam on its closure. The small plane is the last plane to leave Pengam.

Dispatch, Cambrian Air Services, and Messrs. John Curran Ltd. There was also the R.A.F./Civilian manned No.52 Maintenance Unit which was typical of many other units forming in other highly populated areas of the country.

No.52 M.U.

This establishment opened on 3rd of February 1940 as a crating, packaging and shipping depot for single engined aircraft which had to be transported overseas. There were 5 Bellman hangars, two of which were needed for dismantling of aircraft, two for machine and workshops and the fifth for packaging before delivery. Deliveries were undertaken using articulated lorries to the nearby docks at Cardiff, Newport or possibly either Glasgow or Liverpool, or anywhere where a particular plane had to be delivered.

The unit was first named No.43 M.U., but this became confused with 43 Group in messages and phone calls, so it became No.52 M.U. in March 1941. When the site was first opened, there was little equipment. It was at that time at the start of the war, when all the departments of the R.A.F. or indeed all the other services were chasing the same resources. Manpower, especially skills, electrical equipment, machine tools, fuel and timber, steel, catering equipment, beds and furniture. They didn't even have electrical lighting for some time.

The M.U. was under the command of Acting Squadron Leader D. Stacey, the Equipment Officer was Pilot Officer C.R.E. Bridges and the Engineering was Flt. Lt. H.P. Strong. There was a Warrant Officer engineer, Civil Assistant, C.A. and a grade 3 Accountant.

HQ, Equipment, M.T. & A.M. Constabulary Sections 52 M.U. R.A.F Cardiff.

Case Manufacturing, Packing & Blacksmith Sections 52 M.U. Cardiff.

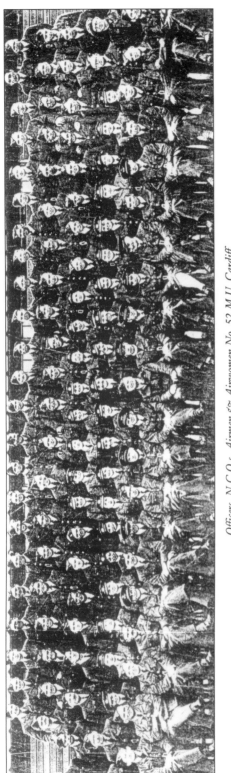

Officers, N.C.O.s, Airmen & Airwomen No. 52 M.U. Cardiff.

Dismantling Section No. 52 M.U. R.A.F. Cardiff.

There is insufficient space in this book to list all the monthly reports for the five years of war, but I shall try to convey a cross section of a month's production.

This progress, even for wartime, is surprising. After scrounging sergeants and airmen and tools from Sealand and other older packaging M.U.'s and searching for timber to make crates at Cardiff's large timber stores Robinsons Davids, John Blands and Edwards and Snook, they were able to get a first delivery of 6x1 inch tongued and grooved 30,000 linear feet. They reported difficulties in finding men for the M.U. from the Labour Exchange and it was a while before men arrived in sufficient numbers. It should be

The Three Bellman hangars on the right comprise 52 M.U.
Carpentry, assembly of crates and dispatching of loaded crates. Pengam Moors.

The Blacksmiths' shop where the steel brackets for lifting by crane and corner plates were forged.

Bellman Hangar used for constructing crates.

The two Bellman hangars for dismantling (Buildings 115 and 116). 52. M.U.

These Hurricane could be bound for the Western desert via Takoradi on the West coast of Africa - many were from 52 M.U.

Hurricanes on arrival at Takoradi after the journey by ship from the UK.

remembered that direction of labour for women had not yet begun.

Below was their first month's arrivals of aircraft:

February 1940	Arrivals	
Hart	7	
Tiger Moth	4	
Audax	4	
Hind	6	
Lysander	5	
Hurricane	21	
Gladiator	12	
Northrop	1	
Sea Gladiator	2	
Total	62	

Despatches	No.	Destination
Hind	2	South Africa
Lysander	6	Headquarters Middle East
Northrops	2	South Africa
Lysander	2	A/C shipping pool for Freetown
Walrus	1	A/C shipping pool for Freetown
Vilderbeest	7	New Zealand
Hurricanes	21	Takoradi
Gladiators	5	South Africa
Tiger Moths	2	Singapore
Audax	1	India
Hart	2	South Africa
Total	51	

The shortage of slinging irons soon showed itself and the numbers of aircraft deliveries increased. The airfield often became unusable because of flooding or sever problems with mud, so that some aircraft were 'nosing in' on landing, or were damaging undercarriages on taking off

The M.U. recruited more and more civilians; mostly over call up age males and some women. They also received more R.A.F. Officers, N.C.O.'s Airmen and Airwomen and the unit gradually expanded.

On one occasion 34 Magisters arrived from 19 M.U. for the Middle East, but there were still shortages of slinging irons. On another occasion 78 Hawker Hinds arrived at South Africa from Sealand; the cases had to be made off site under contract, to be delivered to Cardiff. On 30th March the Fleet Air Arm decided that all their aircraft would be crated and shipped from Cardiff.

Four more articulated lorries were ordered for the unit and timber was in very short supply. No.4 Ferry Pilots Pool was moved to Cardiff because of the output from Air Dispatch and John Currans and the intake into 52 M.U. On 8th May the unit took on 20 extra carpenters, 1 CH carpenter, 1 blacksmith, 1 striker and 6 labourers.

June 1940	Arrivals
Proctors	9
Hinds	26
Walrus	1
Tiger Moth	3
Magister	1
Seafox	2
Albacore	1
Masters	35
Hurricane (Tropical)	38
Gladiators	2
Total	118

Squadron Leader Stacey left for a posting in Belfast, and he was replaced by Squadron Leader P.G. Kirkaldy.

In October 1940 a Harvard No.7122 from 8 M.U. struck one of Cardiff's Balloon Barrage cables on landing. The airscrew and the port side skin were damaged and the cable was cut into the centre section and the cable was cut, but thankfully the plane landed safely. So it went on month after month, the unit getting steadily bigger with more orders and more varied work being introduced besides packing aircraft.

The airfield was still closed to traffic because of the wet boggy conditions for at least a week in each month; the Air Ministry were furious. The airfield needed a hard runway and perimeter track urgently.

October 1940   Delivered
         18 Hurricanes
         2 Vilderbeest
         23 Havards
         1 Vega Gull

October 1941

Production continued never less than 130 A/C/ per month, sometimes 180 per month, but they installed a Sommerfield track across the airfield and it became safer to land and take off, but it was still marshy around the taxiways.

Deliveries
4 Mohawks
3 Albacores
47 Hurricanes
1 Walrus

By now the unit is not only making fuselage crates, wing crates and tail crates for their own orders, but are manufacturing for others. They are also producing wooden items such as trestles, ladders, staging, gun boxes for packing four Browning machine guns per box, A/C chocks, work benches, sand bag boxes, cradles for Rotol Airscrews and undercarriage stands. The M.U. gets bigger and more efficient.

October 1942

Cardiff has now got a concrete runway 960 yards long by 50 yards wide, with concrete perimeter tracks making it safer to land at R.A.F. Cardiff. The deliveries were still going by road to where the ship was docked and that ship was going to the port where the plane was needed. It was a complex procedure to give priority to the aircraft type that had its ship leaving earliest. For example:

October 1942 Despatch

14 Hurricanes	Consignee	Glasgow
32 Hurricanes	Newhouse	Lanarkshire
9 Hurricanes		Southport
6 Hurricanes	Embark	Newport
1 Hurricane	Embark	Swansea
8 Hurricanes	Embark	Cardiff
25 Hurricanes	Embark	Birkenhead
15 Hurricanes	Embark	Liverpool
3 Hurricanes	Embark	Manchester
11 Spitfires	Embark	Newport
1 Battle	Embark	Newport

The M.U. was developing a sports and social aspect in its off duty life. Dances were laid on regularly with football and cricket on the airfield. Lots of local people from Splott, Tremorfa and Pengam who knew one another worked together.

Arrivals October 1942 for despatch

Hurricane MK II B	69 Tropicalised
Hurricane MK II C	65 Tropicalised
Hurricane MK II B/B	23 Tropicalised
Hurricane MK II C/B	3 Tropicalised

Hurricane MK I   9 Tropicalised

Total   169 + 8 Non Trop.

Total 177

August 1944

The airfield at Cardiff had its busiest month.   895 aircraft landed including Dakotas, Cessna Cranes, Bostons, Marauder, Harvards, Noresman, Vengeance Firefly, Vega Gull.

The input from Currans' test flights, Air Dispatch test and deliveries plus the huge increase in the arrivals of Hurricanes, Spitfires and the Fleet Air Arms Seafires. 587 Squadrons' Martinets were also using the runway.

On 31st July 1945 personnel included 123 Airmen, 36 Airwomen and 413 civilians.

Deliveries in July 1945
18 Seafires MK XV
29 Seafires MK III

There were many of these carrier-borne Spitfires boxed up at Pengam's 52 M.U.
during the last years of the War.

August Deliveries
55 Seafires MK XV
30 Seafires MK III
Squadron Leader Kirkaldy was posted to 215 M.U. Dumfries and Squadron Leader W.A. Hart replaced him.

In June 1945 P.O. Tait was in charge of the farm! A farm was created on the land that had been allotments, land that had been purchased by the Air Ministry in the late thirties. At the end of June 1945, the farm had 5 cows which produced 330 gallons of milk each month, 1 bull calf, 31 pigs, a hothouse supplying plants for outside, growing vegetables including tomatoes, beans, cucumbers, peas, broad beans, cabbage, lettuce, onion and leeks. All the messes were kept provided for most of the year.

Further appointments were:
Flight Lt. Ellis ADJ. Officer in charge of Sgts. Mess and P.S.I. and Release Advisory Officer.
Flying Officer Slade in charge of security, discussion groups, Air publications, sport, motor transport admin.
Flying Officer Singleton in charge was Vocational Advisory Officer
Flying Officer James in charge of entertainment
Flying Officer Symonds in charge of sports

The work being undertaken had grown increasingly more varied and sophisticated compared with 1940. Cases for A.A. Mounting Universal 155 off. Undercarriage stands for Spitfires 32 off, prop frames 22 off, spares boxes 20 off, Centauraus engine cases 32 off and packaging sets for Hurricane tail wheel fixing 180 off. Then when the order for shipments of 12 Barracudas arrived, because of the aircraft's design it would require:

Barracuda fuselage cases	12
Barracuda plane cases	12
Barracuda components cases	12
Barracuda props	12
Barracuda spares	6
Barracuda exhaust pipe	12

October 1945
Last entry in the Operations Record Book Air 29 monthly statement.
Deliveries and aircraft handled 140: Barracudas, Dakota, Vega Gull, Beaufort, Traveller and Reliant. Cases for fuselage, planes and tail-plane, ironwork, trestles and map trestles.
On October 31st 1945 52 M.U. R.A.F. Cardiff disbanded.
Two ladies who worked at 52 M.U., both of whom worked in the dismantling hangars illustrate the procedure.

Mrs Iris Neale explains that when a Hurricane was pushed in, a team of four, two men and two women would be assigned. The engine oil and fuel would be dropped and the propellers removed. The wings would be detached and tail-plane removed. When this stripping was complete the aircraft was towed or pushed to the hangars opposite where the crates were made and the aircraft installed on the supports fitted inside the crates.

There were two hangars for dismantling on the eastern side of the apron and three hangars for workshops (carpentry and blacksmiths) and packing on the western side.

Mrs Neal said that the work was very hard. She remarks, 'I've never worked like that before or since. It was cold, there was no heating, but it was a good job done.'

Mrs Vera Anderson said that they worked an eight hour day but if a couple of Hurricane or Spitfires arrived as they were finished for the day, they were told to go home for their evening meal and report back to strip the planes straight away. She also said it was cold most of the time. She agreed it was hard work but enjoyed it. She said that although her home was just the other side of the fence she would be back in the hangar after her lunch to finish her lunch hour with their mates. They would have live music as they had a piano and there were musicians among the R.A.F. lads. They would dance away their lunch breaks. Mrs. Anderson worked there for two and a half years and she enjoyed the company of the men and the women at the M.U. Referring to her dismantling side of the operation, she said that there were only five or six R.A.F. lads working with them, handling mainly undercarriage and guns.

Charge Hand Supervisors were Mick Henley, Joe Clifford and Tom Crother. Chief Carpenter was Len Fishlock. Mrs Anderson said that although Hurricanes were the predominant work when she started there, soon after this changed and it was Spitfires and Seafires.

I have in my possession four large photographs (photocopies) that were in the Operations Record Book of 52 M.U. Each photograph records a section of the workers there. One showing the R.A.F. personnel, there are 119 Officers, N.C.O.'s Airmen and W.A.A.F. on the shot. Another photograph shows the H.Q.M.T.A.M. police and equipment sections showing 96 men and women civilians. The third photograph shows the dismantling section and it adds up to 104 men and women. The fourth photograph reveals the case manufacturing, packaging and blacksmith section adding up to 158 men and women. A total of 477 allowing for any absent, on sick leave and M.T. drivers away on journeys; this unit employed a lot of people.

Cardiff born and Cardiff bred and despite an interest in Pengam Moors all my life, I had regarded the 52 M.U. as a small affair when compared with other production on the airfield, but I was wrong. The M.U. did a big job during a hard time of the war. Most of the buildings and hangars are extant, the only parts of the airfield that is! The headquarters building is now Pengam Moors Social Club. The timber store is now a rack for steel storage. Four of the Bellman hangars have been modified and re-skinned and the fifth is as the original.

John Curran Engineering

Under the auspices of The Civilian Repair Organisation of The Ministry of Aircraft Production in 1940, a purpose built factory for the repair of MK's I, IV & V Blenheims was completed in the massive Curran complex near the bank of the river Taff. During the following five years, the production had reached a total of 193 aircraft including Beaufighters, which had followed on from the Blenheims. They also produced 11,000 extra components such as wings, fuel tanks, engine mountings and under-carriage parts.

The company claims there were 40,000 parts to be examined and it needed 5000 man-hours per plane. The company took over other premises to give more room for the main production line in the new plant. Wings were repaired at a hangar on

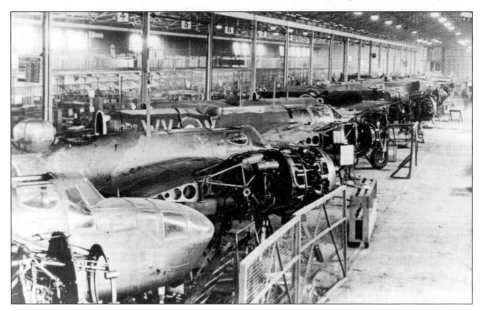

Bristol Blenheim MK IVs on the line at Curran Road Factory.

Pengam Moors belonging to M.A.P. Fuel tanks were repaired and modified at a warehouse on Penarth Road, but the biggest outstation of this company was its hangar/workshop and offices on Pengam (Cardiff) airfield.

The vast majority of sheet metal workers, fitters (engine), fitters (hydraulic), instrument mechanics, electricians, riveters, spray painters and glaziers worked at the main plant. The damaged aircraft would arrive usually on an articulated (Queen Mary) lorry with the wings detached on another 'Queen Mary'. Both props were removed and the wings and props went to the airfield and the aircraft down to the width of this centre section, would be pushed or towed in through the Eastern doors. It would then take its place in line at the end of a queue of Blenheims wide by side, yet at an angle of 20 degrees to each other. At a guess (I did work there for a year), I would say six weeks to two months later it would be in the paint shop.

Then would come the most amazing sight of the whole process. On completion of painting night fighter black, desert browns, blue or home camouflage, it would be towed by the tail and main undercarriage through the streets of Cardiff to Pengam

Blenheims on the assembly line at Curran Road. A Mark IV is on the left and a Mark V is on the right.

The planes were all towed from Curran Road to Pengam Moors where the Flight Shed would assemble the wings to the fuselage, fit the props and test fly from Pengam. This plane is a Blenheim Mark V.

some 3 miles away. The plane would be taken to Currans' Hangar, where it would meet its own wings again. Damaged wings and wing tanks were repaired and brought up to spec and the propellers that had been serviced or replaced were fitted at this time.

Flying controls were then set and engines were run up. When the test pilot became available, he would fly it and snag it then fly it again. This was a short runway at Pengam and it wasn't until mid 1942 that a runway was constructed 960 yds x 50 yds of concrete. Prior to this, the grass airfield could get very muddy and marsh, especially as Pengam Moors is slightly below high tide level to the Severn estuary, and the airfield is surrounded by a sea wall some 10 feet high.

As previously stated, I did work there for a while as a lad of 15yrs until 16 yrs, when I started an apprenticeship with G.W.R. I must say that it was most impressive for me, being a plane buff but I was employed as an instrument stripper/installer and it carried no future in the way of qualifications.

The Bristol Beaufighter contract followed that of the obsolete Blenheim.
Here is the new line of repaired Beaufighters.

The war was going badly in early 1942; Cardiff was bombed fairly regularly between 1941 and 1942. We could get little food and as young people we were grateful for our canteen to supplement our rations. I feel proud to have left school at the age of 14 and undertaken such responsibilities.

Air Dispatch

Another civilian manned aircraft repair facility at Pengam Moors was Air Dispatch Company. The owner of this company was the adventurous record breaker, beautiful socialite The Honourable Mrs Victor Bruce. She had broken records in the air, as

This workshop in Penarth Road 500yds from Curran's main works is where they overhauled and modified Blenheim and Beaufighter wing fuel tanks.

a road race driver, and as a speedboat pilot. Mrs Bruce was married to the fourth son of Lord Aberdare, and he accompanied her on these adventures, in the twenties and thirties. At her death at the age of ninety-four, she still held the records for the fastest return journey from Dover to Calais by motor boat and 17 motoring records, including covering the longest distance for a man or woman 2164 miles in 24 hours. She also held the 24-hour distance covered at sea 674 nautical miles achieved single-handed in 1929. She was the person who had travelled furthest north into Lapland by car.

Amy Johnson, Mrs. V. Bruce and Winifred Spooner at Croydon.

Her flying records include the first solo flight to Japan from England in 1930; the longest solo flight also in 1930; and a record solo flight to French Indo-China from India in 1930. This amazing lady was still racing at Thruxton in the 1970s.

The Hon. Mrs Victor Bruce with her Miles 'Satyr' a one-off design. 1933 air pageant.

The Honourable Mrs Bruce decided to go into the air transport business in the mid thirties. After getting her first D.H. Dragon Rapide, she managed to get the franchise to deliver the London daily newspapers to Paris each early morning.

Mrs. Bruce operated from Heston and ran a profitable airline under the title 'Air Dispatch', so that by September 3rd 1939, she owned no less than twenty three Dragon Rapides, along with the engine fitters, airframe riggers, pilots, navigators and wireless operators to sustain this number of craft. On the 3rd September 1939 The Air

The fleet of D. H. Dragons of Mrs Bruce's Company 'Air Dispatch'.
This shot shows the fleet at the time of impressment for War Service.

Ministry delivered a brown sealed envelope into Mrs Victor Bruce's hands, that had been planned and composed the previous week. It told her that her company was to be mobilised and that ten of her D.H. Rapides were to be confiscated into the R.A.F. She and her remaining fleet were to depart to Cardiff (Pengam Moors) immediately. This she did and as a result The National Air Communications Unit was formed.

Her planes were doing all kinds of jobs during the so-called phoney war, mostly flying to Paris and other continental destinations of V.I.P.'s and top ranking officers of the three services.

When France fell, these flights ceased so The Air Ministry commandeered her aircraft and The Air Ministry threatened to take her craftsmen for the M.A.P. (The Ministry of Production).

Being the resourceful woman that she was, and knowing the right people, she was given a two-week period to acquire a Ministry of Defence contract, to build or repair aircraft in order to keep her skilled workforce and her hangar. Within a week she had secured a contract from Helliwells Ltd., which comprised of 40 wings which were fabric covered and were taken from training aircraft to be repaired. When this contract was completed to the satisfaction of M.A.P. she received orders for hundreds of wings, and fuselages and ultimately whole aircraft.

So it continued with the biplane family of Hawkers, Harts, Furies, Audax etc, all to be finished as trainers. This proved to be the basis for her thriving business until she received orders to repair damaged North American Harvards in the U.K. in 1943 which lasted until 1945.

While this main production was going on there were many other sideline contracts,

Under a block of flats at Westgate St was the scene where
aircraft wings and tailplanes were doped and painted.

Air Dispatch basement, Westgate St. The light from windows to the right is a view overlooking Cardiff Rugby Ground and the River Taff.

such as the maintenance and modification of Vultee Vengeance dive or Torpedoe Bombers, or the unpacking and assembly of numerous Curtiss Seamew sea planes for the U.S. Navy. The Seamew was a ship borne reconnaissance aircraft carried by Capital ships.

They also had contracts for large numbers of pontoons for use in Japan. The company also had contracts for cowlings and nacelles for Lysanders and Wellingtons.

Air Despatch had three areas of production: No.1 hangar on the airfield, the M.A.P. hangar (near Currans' hangar), and the huge basement below the executive block of flats that overlook Cardiff Arms Park. At its peak the company employed 700 people, the hangars are long gone, so they are identified from old photos.

The basement of the prestigious block of flats in Westgate St., Cardiff served Air Dispatch for five busy years in the repair & maintenance of mostly single engine trainers.

The North American 'Harvard' provided most of the work in the later years of the War.

The basement is now a public car park. When the war ended the work ceased and the Hon. Mrs.Bruce tried to return her company to running an airline. But it was not to be. The new socialist government thought that Britain had to nationalise the airlines under the flags of British Overseas Airways and European Airways and the rest were brushed aside. So once again this lady had to start all over again. She had amassed a very skilled army of carpenters and sheet metal workers; even the female trainees had developed into good benders and riveters of duralumin etc. She had the hangars, workers and machines, so she applied to The Lancashire Coach Works to tender for a contract to build the bodies for trolley buses that were at just that time being delivered to Cardiff Bus Company.

Air Dispatch were successful at coach building, so much so that they built the coaches for several other Corporations in addition to Cardiff. The company round about now changed its name to Bruce Coachwork and did well until a shortage of aluminium slowed them down until it all became uneconomical and the company was forced to cease activities in the late fifties.

Cardiff Corporation Bus made by Air Dispatch at Pengam Moors. December 1947.

I have spoken to lots of men and women who worked for Air Dispatch and they all said that they enjoyed the work, were treated fairly and in some cases they didn't mind going to work at all. Here are examples from some of the workers:

Rick Moore comments: I was 15 years old and a trainee on engines, mostly out on the apron in all weathers. We had a lot of Yanks flying in, in their Beechcraft and wearing their pinks and gabardines, looking to get work done (1944). We had Thunderbolts, Vengeances and Bostons. The one Yank who was there the most gave me a leather jacket with an eagle on the back, my son has it now.'

Ken Rapson (sheet metal worker) remarks: I started in 1941 at the age of 14 and by 1942 I was making the lovely engine nacelles for the Hawker Fury & Hart. I learned to use jigs and I was never afraid of a job no matter what its shape.'

The company had visits from the boss. She would fly in frequently from London with the Managing Director Mr Vickers and when these two walked through the factory everyone got on with their work.

The manager at Pengam Moors was Mr Dunbar, the manager at Westgate Street basement as Mr Nichols, and the personnel manager was Mr Pembridge, Chief Inspector was Mr Jewel and test pilots at various periods were Mr Dick Evans from Glosters and Mr Peter Clifford.

Heath Park

Another airfield in the leafy suburbs of Cardiff for a short spell was at Heath Park. When the American army moved over here in preparation for D-Day, they occupied many sites in Cardiff. Maindy Barracks, Whitchurch Common and Heath Camp were the busiest.

In the summer of 1943 ten Piper Cub L4 Grasshoppers were shipped over from the

Cardiff Corporation Trolley Bus made by Bruce Coachwork, Pengam Moors.

Guard Room, Heath Camp, or as the Americans called it 'Camp Heath' (2000)

U.S.A. along with other munitions to Cardiff Docks. After unloading these aircraft that were in a crated form, they were transported by road to Pengam Moors, where they were installed in the John Currant flight shed. After assembly by the U.S. Army engineers they stayed at the airfield for a few months, and then they were flown to their allocated units, including the Glider field at Llanishen and Heath Camp, both in Cardiff.

This is the Drill Hall, 'Camp Heath' still in use today.

Heath Camp. The landing ground was established on removal of the hedge line seen upper left. There were at least two Piper Cubs based here up to D-Day and briefly afterwards.

The U.S. army had arrived in the early spring of 1944 at what the U.S. army called 'Camp Heath' bringing with them a Battalion of Field Artillery. And they were to be the recipients of at least two of the Grasshoppers for A.O.P. (Air Observation Posts). These planes needed to have the airstrip as close to the battalion headquarters as possible so they used the field at the northern side of the park used today as football pitches. All this was great fun for the local lads as there were no restriction on the use of the field by the public.

The pilots of these small planes were expert at landing and taking off in small spaces, but Heath Park's largest uninterrupted treeless space was still less than 400 yards. And they would only just clear Heath Park Avenue's houses by a few feet.

Just before D-Day, they simply vanished and it lay quiet until November 1944 when a back-up division for the continent, the 75th Infantry Division brought its own artillery spotter L4s to 'Camp Heath'. They stayed for a brief period before, they too vanished, never to be seen again. Heath Park had had its moment in aviation history.

This Piper Cub is not only typical of those at Heath Park but actually saw War Service on the continent. It is owned by Ken Wakefield. (courtesy of Mr. Ken Wakefield).

Cub strip Heath Park. Northerly aspect.

Glider Field Llanishen

Another landing ground for light aircraft was temporarily established at Llanishen during the war. This substantial area of council land was largely earmarked for housing and industrial development post-war, in 1941, it was a large fairly flat area bounded by Ty Glas Road in the north, Kimberley Road and Coed y Cae woods to the east, the Crystal woods and the railway to the south.

The Inland Revenue offices and other industry such as Royal Ordnance's large site were to the west.

In early 1941 the Air Training Corps were allowed to use this area to fly and land gliders as part of the lads' training in handling powered aircraft. In the beginning they

An R.A.F. overhead photograph of the Glider Field in 1948. The blister hangar can be seen just on the north of the road with the Viscosuisse Factory being built on the other side of the road. Now known as Ty-Glas Avenue.

relied on a saloon car to give them tows to become airborne, the car was a gift from a local businessman. Later the A.T.C. acquired a fine improvement as a tug. It was a mobile, balloon barrage winch, the same as the winches manned by the W.A.A.F.S. around the city at that time.

The lads carried on their flying weather permitting; they received a visit from the famous bomber leader Guy Gibson (whose wife lived in Penarth) in 1943 to give the lads

A typical example of Air Training Corps during the War.

a pep talk. Then came the news that the unit had to move out to Pengam Moors air-field to continue their flying room there, as the Yanks were coming.

The Americans brought three Piper Cubs and used the blister hangars that had been erected for the A.T.C.'s gliders to house and maintain them. The soldiers serv-icing the aircraft were in tented accommodation along the rear of Ty Glas Road. The hangars were at the North East corner of the landing ground near to the tax offices.

Just a few days before D-Day on 6th June 1944, the Americans left - an event repeated all over the U.K.

Today the Glider Field is only a corner of the area of the war. The leisure centre,

This is a Piper Cub as would have been seen at the Glider Field in Llanishen in 1943/44.
The Leisure Centre occupies some of the airstrip.

offices and warehouses cover nine tenths of it; just a small contribution but impor-tant. It has been said that the light aircraft that were lodged temporarily at this field were a part of the 2nd Evacuation Unit which was based on Whitchurch Common, the period last 1943 to June 1944. They were also living in tents on an area of the

Common on the south side of Merthyr Road extending to an area where the houses of Clos Corner and Heol Coed Cae were later to be built. The unit had its mess hall and admin on the opposite side of Merthyr Road next to Ararat Chapel. The proof needed to verify that the glider field was the flying connection with the 2nd Evac. Unit remains speculation.

It has been alleged that the 2nd Evac. Unit based on Whitchurch Common made use of the Glider Field for VIP Medical Staff and L4 Sentinal Ambulance Trials. yet no proof is available and the US Army use was confined to AOP with the Artillery Units.

This is the only remaining piece of grass at the Glider Field Llanishen, Cardiff.

1945 - present day

Pengam Moors Cardiff Airport No. 7 Motor Transport Company 54 Wing

Early in 1945 as the European conflict came to an end, 7MT Co. was formed at Pengam to strip every Welsh region airfield of all that could be moved by road, and those items of furniture, tools, machines, tractors, wireless equipment and cooking gear to be sold. In fact, every large load was moved by No.7. The loads were dumped at various sites, some drivers say that they used the one dump, others say they used many different ones.

The dumps were at Stamford Bridge (Lincs), Quedgeley (Glous), Spanhoe, and Speke. The fleet of vehicles was substantial. The articulated fleet was split equally between Queen Mary and they heavy trailers with four sets of two tyres on a strong trailer, pulling these were Bedford and Commer units. Heavy lorries including Scammells, Diamond T's, Matadors and Thornycrofts formed the remainder of the company.

7 M.T. Company orderly room, Newport Road, Cardiff.

The garage at Albany Road, Cardiff that was commandeered by the R.A.F. as it had a powerful hydraulic lift and other equipment.

7 Motor Transport Company at the end of the War, when 52 MU had closed, the next tenant of this Bellman was 7 MT Comp Headquarters. It is the middle of three hangars. Much renovated.

No.7 MT Company was based at the Bellman Hangar No. 106 on the airfield site plan. It is the middle of three Bellmans that up until then had been packing Seafires. This hangar had offices inside and was the headquarters of the unit, under the command of Squadron Leader W.H. Herbert.

There was another office in a private residence in Newport Road Cardiff. It being

A.E.C. Matador No7 MT Company.

3 Ton Bedford No. 7 MYC

described to me as the orderly room and administration under the command of Flt. Lieutenant W.E.Smith. The unit took over the garage in Albany Road Cardiff belonging to a Mr Sydney Jones because it had a huge hydraulic vehicle lift, also a forklift truck that was very rare in those days. The garage is still there but it is closed and becoming derelict. Because of the size and numbers, the vehicles were dispersed at various locations in a small radius from the airfield. These locations were:

A Big Nose Bedford

A Queen Mary articulated truck of No.7 Motor Transport Company.

1. A yard at Wern Fawr farm on what was then the A48 (now B4487), on the western side of the road, just beyond St. Mellons on the Cardiff eastern boundary. This yard is built upon now and cannot be traced. The yard accommodated the heavy trailers known as Alan Taylors with 4 x 2 wheels for the carriage of crates and heavy equipment. Tug units were mainly Crossleys and Bedfords.
2. The large yard at The Farmers and Dairymen on Newport Road was used for the large trucks.
3. The hangar at Pengam Moors 52MU site was home to lighter vehicles.

Those men who were not married and without a local home to go to, used the barracks

Tractor Diamond T. No. 7 Motor Transport Company.

huts on the airfield. The reason that a large number of men were of local addresses is because the whole company was comprised of men waiting for their turn for demobilisation.

I have spoken to local men who were in India driving these types of lorries and then arrived at Liverpool in late 1945 to be posted to Cardiff Pengam to join this new unit. A lot of aircrew were also diverted to No.7 MT, those who couldn't drive

7 M.T. Company - Farmers and Dairyman Yard. Used by 82 (The Mid Heavy) Trailer Contingent.

The first post-war commercial flight. Cambrian Air Services used an Auster Autocrat.
(Captain Ken Wakefield).

because of the lack of licences were riding as mates to the drivers. There were too many motor fitters and mechanics, and as one extremely experienced fitter said that he volunteered to go driving because he was bored with getting in one another's way. The idea was to put men aircrew, ground crew or whatever as near to their homes as possible until demobilisation. The date of late 1947 has been generally agreed as the wind up of this unit.

Cambrian resumed flying on 1st January 1946. The pilot Mr Symmons of Cambrian flew a hired Auster 'Autocrat' from Cardiff to Bristol (Filton), there were no passengers aboard, only cargo. This was the first post-war commercial flight by any one, upon the lifting of restrictions by the Ministry of Transport.

In 1947 the company owned 3 Austers, G-AGVU, G-AGYT and G-AIGY. (All Autocrats), a Proctor 1 G-AHEV and a Hendy Heck, G-AEMR. In 1948 they purchased the Autocrat that they had hired for the first post war flight, but the most important buy was the D.H.Dragon Rapide G-AGZJ, with room for six passengers. With a staff of three pilots, the company went into charters, aircraft maintenance and air photography.

One regular charter was the pleasure flying of holidaymakers, mostly from Butlins holiday camp at Pwllheli providing the customers, flying from an airfield called Broomhall.

Dragon Rapide of Cambrian Air Services. 'Anglesey' outside Bellman hangar at Pengam.

Government moves after the war attempted to eradicate all the small airlines of this country, giving the virtual monopoly to British European Airways of all local regional flights, but it didn't work so well for the state airline, as they simply could not make some of these destinations pay. Cambrian did not pay the same salaries, or have the same overheads as B.E.A. and could make a profit on a route, whereas the large bureaucratic company was not as competitive. So, B.E.A. gave the Cardiff to Weston route to Cambrian, in association with Western Airways. Cambrian used its Rapides G-AKUB, G-AKUC and G-AGZJ. Western used Anson. This arrangement only lasted a year as Western pulled out in the summer of 1949, leaving the way for Cambrian to begin its rise that would eventually make it the largest independent air company in the U.K.

Cambrian were pleased later in 1949 that the Air Transport Advisory Council awarded what was renamed Cambrian Airways, licences to operate to Jersey, Guernsey, Barnstaple, London and Birmingham. The plum route was the Channel Islands but

Aero_Club at Cardiff Post-War. The aircraft seen is the 'Autocrat' and 'Tipsy'.

Pengam Moors 'Battle of Britain' Day 20th Sept 1947. Airspeed 'Consul' is in the foreground.

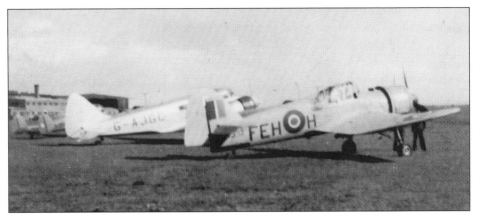

Master II EM 392 at Pengam Moors 'Battle of Britain day' 20 Sept 1947.
Consul and Gemini in background.

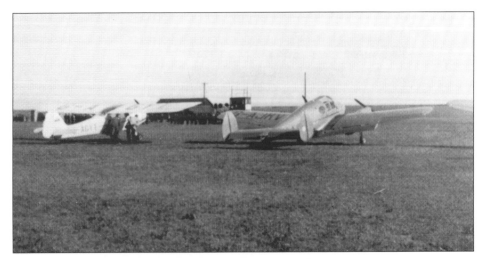

Pengam Moors 'Battle of Britain day' 20 Sept 1947. Gemini and Autocrat.

Cambrian Air Services D.H. Dove over the Glamorgan coast. (Captain Ken Wakefield)

they could not get Cardiff to Dublin. It was now necessary to buy three more Rapides G-ALAT, G-ACLE and G-ALRW. The inaugural flight to Jersey on 16th May 1949 was in a Dragon Rapide G-AGZJ.

In 1950 the manager and chief pilot was Bill Elwin who at that time had staff of three engineers, three pilots and three office workers. During his stay of nineteen years it grew to over 130 pilots and a total staff of approximately 1,000.

The first internal Welsh service was provided by B.E.A. not Cambrian. On the 11th April 1949 B.E.A. inaugurated a service between Cardiff and Valley in Anglesey. There was one return service a day for six days a week. However the route, which

This was the departure bay at Pengam until the move to Rhoose.
One of these Doves was off to Paris, the other to Jersey.

included Liverpool and Hawarden proved uneconomic and was closed down on 1st October after averaging only 1.8 passengers per flight. Later the world's first Helicopter service linking Cardiff to Wrexham and Liverpool was operated by B.E.A. with Cambrian the handling agents. Money was always tight at Cambrian, and it needed aircraft with larger payloads to bring in more money. This was a problem as larger aircraft meant longer runways. What was suitable for the D.H.Doves and Rapides was not suitable for Dakotas or Viscounts.

The old R.A.F. runway of 960 x 50 yds needed lengthening to a minimum of 1,300 yards. The estimated price was £120,000 and was only giving the company the opportunity to operate the Dakotas and Viscounts. When it came to operate the faster and heavier jet airliners coming into service they would need a much longer runway.

Cambrian made an offer to Haverfordwest and Swansea Councils to take over the management of their wartime airfields (Withybush and Fairwood Common) so that the airlines could use them after some clearing up of the sites. This was agreed by all concerned, so a base was established out to the western end of the service. To do this Captain Keeble was stationed at Haverfordwest as manager, living in the control tower, and he flew a daily service to and from Cardiff. He was joined by Ray Boutcher to maintain the Rapide G-ALZJ that was based there. This service did not last long, and Captain Keeble returned to Cardiff. A similar situation occurred when Captain R.de Wilde, whose home was in Cheltenham, became manager of the airport at Staverton under Cambrian and took over the running of the airport and flew a Rapide service to and from Whitchurch to link up with the Cardiff, Bristol, Southampton, Paris and the Cardiff, Bristol, Guernsey, Jersey services in 1953 to 1956. On 9th April 1950 Cambrian started a link with Liverpool. Wing Commander Bill Elwin, General Manger, piloted the D.H. Rapide with eight passengers from Speke Airport to Cardiff. This was the start of a long association of Cambrian with Liverpool.

On 13th March 1951 the founder of the company told the board that he had been appointed a Director of B.E.A. and as a result of this he had to resign from the position of Managing Director of C.A.S.

The company expanded further, and in 1953 bought two more Rapides G-AGSI and G-AIYE and three Doves G-AIWF, G-AKSK and G-AIYE. These aircraft were purchased in a deal with Moreton Air and Olley Air service, which also included two Consuls that were never operated by Cambrian. They were sold on a long time later. At this time the Chief Engineer was 'Dinty' Moore (Laurie), Asst. Engineer was Doug Sumers. Engineer staff were Wilf Brunsdon, Ray Boutcher, Ken Peat, Percy Smith and Ted Sawyer.

In 1954 a Dakota G-AMSW was bought from Air Service Training at Hamble for type rating. At this period the pilots were Bill Elwin, Ronnie de Wilde, Arthur Townsend, Geoff Perrott, Geo. Keeble, Ken Wakefield, John Gibson and Lionel Roberts.

Then on 1st April 1954 all Civil Airline flying was transferred to Rhoose as Cardiff had become not only too short, but also building work was planned on the periphery of the airport which would impede the flight path.

The first interruption to the history of Cambrian was due to the Second World War. This second interruption was due to the total change in its base - twelve miles to the west of Cardiff at the village of Rhoose.

The No. 1 Fire Fighting School at Pengam Moors, Cardiff.

Started January 1st 1948 and closed late 1961.

The school started with four new recruits and four Fire Officers, all employed as civilians for The Ministry of Transport and Civil Airways. They went to many airfields in order to collect pieces of unwanted aircraft, to enable a start to be made at the technique of fighting an aircraft fire. Manston in Kent supplied a lot of material from the wartime emergency runway. For most of the following year little was done to start bringing in pupils, because these four men and four officers developed the first techniques of aircraft fire suppression.

During the war the officers had learned the hard way of how to tackle R.A.F. aircraft fires, and now as civilians they used their experience of how best to extinguish civil aircraft fires. By January 1949 they took in the first batch of pupils for sixteen-week courses. The schoolrooms and canteen were in R.A.F. huts, one of which is

Bedford Q.L. No.1 Fire Fighting School.

No. 1 Fire Fighting School Pengam.

today the St Albans Social Club. The students billeted in the houses in Whittaker Street and in other streets near the airfield. In the early years a fire dump was situated on the foreshore of The Bristol Channel outside the southern perimeter of he airfield which was later moved nearer to inside the southern perimeter track.

By now on charge were two Thornycroft Fire Tenders, two Bedford Q.L. Army lorries for foam and water tankers, Austin gas trucks carrying 12no. 60lb. C.O.2 cylinders, a wide nosed Bedford 1,000 gallon tanker with a Rolls Royce B18 main engine and many other smaller vehicles. The officers in charge were Harry Radford Lucas O/C, Bill McDonald Chief Instructor, Asst. D.N.Officer Mr P Friend and Instructor Bill Stapleton.

The firemen on the staff at Pengam changed somewhat as men retired or changed jobs but here is a list some of the men that handled the appliances and drove the vehicles at Pengam. They were Mr. Ken Griffiths, Mr. Ivor (Tug) Wilson, Mr. Noel Weston, Mr.

Halifax on the fire dump at Pengam.

No. 1 Fire School at Stansted after leaving Pengam.

Noel Parkins, Mr. Chris Gee, Mr. Dennis Emmet, Mr. Parmeter and Mr. Kytlie.

The Pupils arrived from all over the U.K., The Empire and Dominions, Europe, The Middle East, West Africa and India. In fact any major airport in any country needed to know how high octane petrol and jet engine kerosene needed a different technique in the event of aircraft crashes and fires and how to cope with the fabrics

No. 1 Fire School at Stansted after leaving Pengam.

This memorial was erected by members of the 614 Sq Association. It is in honour of those members who died in action, and is placed half way down the runway in what is now parkland on Pengam Moors.

and upholstery of an airliner on fire. In some cases the water tender was needed but usually the foam tender was used and in some situations a saturation of CO_2 did the trick!

In the training, staff and pupils made use of the fire dump even though they only had bits and pieces of aircraft to practice on. Then De Havilland's at Hatfield gave the school a D.H.Comet that had made the exhaustive vibration tests for metal fatigue and was of course no longer any use as an airliner. Then along came a H.P.Hasting fuselage (some firemen say two Hastings) and a Seafire. The course was now of one month's duration and was fully booked at all times, perhaps forty men at each course. The staff of course went home when not on duty and the Chief Instructor lived on site to cover emergencies.

The permanent staff numbered ten or twelve at any one time until 1955, when Pengam, having closed down, moved all its civil operations to Rhoose some 12 miles away, and some of the firemen were also sent there to satisfy the needs of safety at the airport. The instructors and a couple of firemen were left until The Rover Transmission factory started building; they packed up and the school moved to Stansted in Essex in 1961.

Machine Products factory built at the same time as the
Air Ministry bought and built on the land for 614 Sq.

The school began in 1948 under auspices of Ministry of Transport and Civil Airways, and then it changed to Ministry of Civil Aviation then Ministry of Aviation then Board of Trade and finally Civil Airways Authority. It is believed that the school now moved from Stansted in 1970 to Teeside (Middleton St George) having been privatised under the name of 'Serco'. There is no argument that this school was the very first of its kind. It was born out of the urgent need for the U.K. to lead in all things

Tesco Store built on the southern part of the flying field at Pengam Moors.

aviation at the War's end. To make foreign earnings and for prestige it was the yard-stick for other countries.

The school would probably still be at Cardiff now, if it had not had to move to make way for the new Rover Works, as it did not need an airfield to function. Most pupils loved going to Pengam as the local amenities such as The Ocean Club (where every pupil was made an honorary member) and the closeness of Cardiff City Centre, with its shops and entertainment. Not to mention the excellent food served in the canteen by Ma Griff who was known and loved from Shannon to Nairobi. And, especially as the pupils were called back to Pengam after six months for a refresher course.

The radio call sign in emergencies was 'Southdown' and this was used a few times while the school was at Pengam. In the summer of 1959 a D.H. Dove belonging to L.E.C. refrigeration, was circling the city as a joy ride for visiting businessmen. It lost the use of an engine and crashed on North Road, a busy residential area. 'South-down' was called to attend the incident, but sadly three lives were lost. Another incident occurred in the Penhill area of the city, where a Gloster Meteor crashed in a field bounded by an hotel and a girls' school.

The date of closure of the school was 1955 although the upper echelon survived until 1961.

Miles Master MK1

A Spitfire MK II of 53 Operational Training Unit R.A.F. Rhoose.

R.A.F. Rhoose / Cardiff International Airport

ST064674   3mls West of Barry   Sth Glam.   Nr. B4265/A4226

When Llandow opened as an A.S.U. (Aircraft Storage Unit) on 1/4/40 it was called upon to host a training unit also. This was happening to other storage and Maintenance Units as the need to evacuate these schools to areas away from intervention form the Luftwaffe was urgent. Not only did this allow the trainee pilots to apply their attention exclusively to their work, but it freed up airfields in the south east to operational squadrons.

In Llandow's case the outfit that they were allocated was No.53 Operational Training Unit. And as in most cases this meant that a Satellite airfield was necessary near-

Martinet Target Tug.

by, to share the workload on Llandow's facilities. That was why Rhoose was built.

The site of this airfield was a few hundred yards from the east to the south at Rhoose village, and to the north the village of Penmark. It was completed and opened on 7/4/42 to the relief of all at Llandow.

The arrival of B Flight of 53 O.T.U. at Llandow on 24/6/41 had left A&C flights at Heston where they were to form No.61 O.T.U. With B flights flown in the H.Q. and the main party arrived on 1/7/41. With 27 plus 9 MK I Spitfires, 10 plus 4 Masters and 3 Targets towers, all under the control of No. 81 Group.

The trainees used Rhoose from its opening as the runways were so busy at Llandow, but there was little hangarage or accommodation, so the maintenance of the aircraft was done at the parent base.

So hundreds of the British, Canadian, Australian and New Zealanders, did their combat training, dog fighting in the skies of Glamorgan for the two year of their tenancy of Rhoose, and many of these lads died or were badly injured in this deadly game.

By 1943 it was clear that the air field at Rhoose was poorly laid out, and was responsible for many accidents and injuries, and planning was afoot to relieve some of the growing congestion with the continuous takes offs and landings, as the establishment of the unit was now 56 plus 19 in reserve Spitfires 17 plus 5 in reserve Masters, and 4 plus 2 Target towers.

Mr Hugh Trivett has provided me with some facts on the casualties on 53 O.T.U. shared between Llandow and Rhoose. At least 92 Spitfires lost. 50 written off Cat.E. 14 damaged but repairable Cat B., and about 8 in the sea. The fate of the remainder is unknown as the records at the Air Historical Branch of the M.O.D. went missing many years ago.

The majority of the spitfires used at the O.T.U. were war weary and worn, before joining the unit. The Spitfires on service here regularly crashed in to the mountains north of the airfield, some of the which rise to 2,000 feet, collided with other aircraft, both in the air and on take off and landing, stalling and spinning for example on 7th July 1941: Spitfires X4024 and X4607, collided during a training session. X4024 crashed on a house in Mount Pleasant, Merthyr killing several people and the Canadian pilot Sgt. G.F.Manuel. X4607 crashed in a field between Mount Pleasant and Quaker's Yard, killing the pilot Sgt. L.Goldberry R.C.A.F. Both of these aircraft had flown in the Battle of Britain with 92 Squadron.

On the 9th of July 1941 Spitfire N3230 crashed and burnt out. This had flown in the Battle of Britain with 64 Squadron. Also 9th July, Spitfire P9383 crashed and burnt out at Colwinston killing the pilot Sgt. F.G.T. McGahy. This aircraft also few in the Battle of Britain with No.616 Squadron.

On 10th July 1941, X4988 during dog fighting practice, attempted an upward roll, fell into a spin, recovered and flicked into another spin and crashed at Marcross aerodrome at 15.30hrs. The pilot M.A.Plomteau R.C.A.F is buried at Llantwit Major.

During August 6th 1941 Spitfire X4381 was on a general training flight when the starboard wing broke away during a dive. The aircraft crashed into a hill near Ton

Pentre killing the pilot Flt. Lt.M.A.Goodwin, an ex Battle of Britain Spitfire that flew with 152 Squadron.

On the 12th August 1941 Spitfire R7057 came out of cloud and flew at 1960 feet into Graig-y-Llyn, Pen-y-Cae, above Rhigos at 1900hrs killing the pilot Pilot Officer C.J.Day R.A.F.V.R.

The 26th August 1941 saw Spitfire X4263 crash at Rhoose point at 1315 hrs killing the pilot Sgt. J.P. Mac Ilwane. Another Battle of Britain Spitfire with 603 Squadron.

On 22nd September 1941 Spitfire K9976 stalled and spun after a steep dive and crashed near St Mary Church Flemingstone killing the pilot Sgt. R.E.Murray R.C.A.F.

Also on 11th September Spitfire 9930 was abandoned by the pilot Sgt. Cresswell due to a jammed aileron and it crashed near Lake Farm Cowbridge. The pilot was unhurt. The plane was ex Battle of Britain which was flown with 152 Squadron.

Spitfire N3198 on 15th September 1941 Force landed and crashed at Llandow and was struck off charge.

25th September 1941 Spitfire L1054 dived into the sea a ½ mile south east of Llantwit Major killing the pilot Sgt. G.F.Parker.

These are just a few of the O.T.U.'s early disasters but the carnage continued until No.53 O.T.U.'s days in Wales ceased when the whole unit was transferred to Kirton-in-Lindsay on 9th May 1943. The airfield at Rhoose lay quiet for ten months, then the place was made ready in something of an emergency for the intake of another unit.

No. 7 Gunnery School

This Unit had been based at Stormy Down since the beginning of the War, but the poor airfield surface had caused many accidents and extensive repairs, drainage and the building of a hard runway was needed there. While this was being done No.7 Gunnery School was moved temporarily to Rhoose. On Tuesday 8th February 1944, 23 Ansons, 20 Martinets, and 50 pilots moved ten miles or so eastward to continue

Avro Anson Gunnery Trainer as used at No. 7 AGS Rhoose.

Rhoose was in this configuration by 1944. (Air Photo Reproduction. Ord.Survey. N:C:00/639.)

their drogue towing and firing along the same coast lines as before.

Target tugs of No.587 Squadron Anti-aircraft Co-op. were also using Rhoose and it was somewhat busy on the airfield, so orders were issued that to prevent collisions all 7 A.G. aircraft were to have airmen at the wing tips when taxi-ing.

There was a change to the establishment on April 27th 1944, six Ansons were added making 27 for use and 10 in reserves plus two dual control machines. Martinets were reduced by seven to total 18 with ten reserve. On the 1st of May three Ansons arrived from No.9 (O) A.F.U. Penrhos to complete the strength.

On 4th May Sgt. E. Janiszewski (Polish) in Martinet JN 420 ran out of fuel on his approach to drop a sleeve on Rhoose. He force landed safely on the airfield.

May 7th saw Martinet MS836 (587 Squadron). The engine cut out on take off. The aircraft ran through the perimeter fence into a field and turned over. The crew was unhurt.

Four days later 587 Squadron aircraft attached of target duties on Thornbury Maritime Royal Artillery School range, returned to Cardiff (Pengam Moors).

Monday 8th May was a black day for 7 A.G.S. with 8 deaths. Three Ansons took off from Rhoose on Cinegun exercise with a Martinet. Ansons LV300 and MG131

Martinet target tow at Rhoose with No.7 Air Gunners School.

collided about 1 ½ miles out at sea from Porthcawl Point. The Duty Boat put to sea but found only an empty dinghy and some wreckage. Eventually all the bodies were found and buried at Nottage.

The month of June began with a taxi accident when Flt. Sgt. Foes in Martinet JN419 hit an open door on a bowser. On the 18th the same Sgt. took off in Martinet MS675 with LAC Stover as target operator. His engine seized at 1,500 feet and he made a good landing at Rhoose. Swinging to avoid parked aircraft he hit a picket block and the undercart collapsed.

Suddenly news arrived that because of the reduction in training requirements, the air gunner schools were to be re-organised - No.7 A.G.S. was to disband by September 2nd 1944 and No. 8 A.G.S. at Evanton by August 28th.

Other units affected were No.1 at Pembrey, No.2 at Dalcross, No.3 at Castle Kennedy, were to have pupil capacities of 360 each. 4 A.G.S. Morpeth, and 11 A.G.S. at Andreas were to have 240 each. Capacity at 10 A.G.S. Barrow as to be 240 W.O.P./A.G. at Bishop's Court 12 A.G.S. they would receive 160 Flt. Eng. and Flt. Mech. Trainees No.9 (O) A.F.U. were to hold up 120 Ags.

On 2nd August all aircraft returned from Rhoose to Stormy Down and preparations were made to close Rhoose down. It was transferred to No.40 Group, Maintenance Command on November 1st becoming a sub-site of 214 M.U. at Newport and used for storage. When 59 M.U. formed at Newland Gloucestershire, with a detached site at Rhoose an explosive storage unit from 6/6/45 and on 15/4/46 the whole unit moved to Rhoose from Newland. It disbanded on 29/2/47.

Strangely the airfield had reached its best configuration at the end of No. 7 A.G.S.'s tenure. The runways had comprised a simple cross at the middle of the field, but now the extension to the North –East to South-West runway from 1100 yards to 1560 yards and the improved peri-track association with it enabled aircraft to move without impeding other aircraft. The other runway 13/31 S.E. to N.W. received no extension at this time, but in years to come would be developed into the main runway for the Cardiff International Airport. There had never been excess maintenance hangars here, just four enlarged Blister hangars on the Northern hardstands.

A small Watch Office of brick was positioned inside the southern peri-track. Adjacent to runway southeast to northwest 13/31 the runway northeast to southwest was extended in 1944.

Rhoose had by now built up a fair showing of domestic sites; the usual airmen, sergeants and officers' sleeping sites on one side of the road and the W.A.A.F.'s well away on

Early days at Rhoose. Departure facilities on the Rhoose Village side of the airfield.

Cambrian Dakotas, Rhoose.

the other, also a communal site, sick quarters and the usual messes.

While 53 O.T.U. were here their aircraft were serviced at Llandow. When No.7 A.G.S. occupied the airfield servicing of their aircraft was carried out at Stormy Down.

With the disbanding of the bomb store of 59 M.U. and the sub-site of 214M.U. the airfield closed approximately January 1948 and the place lay dormant for four years.

In the early fifties the Irish State Airline Aer Lingus had been trying hard to set up a route between Dublin and Cardiff and Cardiff's airport was still at Pengam Moors. This was not an airport that could handle the Aer Lingus D.C.3's and at that time there was much discussion on the future of Pengam as planning permission was about to be passed allowing the building of a mini steelworks in the runway's path.

Special arrangements were made for Aer Lingus to use Rhoose. Ground staff were switched to Rhoose for each individual movement starting in 1952. The Ministry of Transport and Civil Aviation were drawn in and by 1954 all operations including those of Cambrian Airways were transferred to Rhoose.

Conditions were primitive. The R.A.F. base had been allowed to become almost derelict, and there was no sanitation. The M.T.C.A. spent £30,000 on strengthening and resurfacing the runways. The wartime buildings were converted into terminal buildings and a T2 Hangar was brought from Withybush Airfield (Haverfordwest) at a cost of £100,000.

In June 1952 the first service by Aer Lingus form Dublin to Rhoose was inaugurated with a D.C.3 and by the end of the first year of operations, carried nearly 6000 passengers between the two Cities. In 1969 (the year ending in March) 15,000 passengers and 108,000 kilos of freight were carried between Ireland and South Wales alone. In fact, at that time it was the best route to America from the South Wales area. Daily flights linked Cardiff to Dublin and the company's Boeing Jet network from Dublin to New York, Boston, Chicago and Montreal.

The company introduced B.A.C. 111's and Boeing 737's on the Cardiff to Dublin route in 1970 but inexplicably dropped the route in the mid seventies.

This route was snapped up by Manx Airlines and Ryanair who both still operated from Cardiff. Manx was incorporated into British Regional Airways.

When Cambrian Air Services was forced to leave Pengam Moors Airport they joined Aer Lingus at Rhoose two years later in 1954 flying the D.C.3's .

The company sold off its five Rapides and started work with the two Dakotas brought from Staverton. Using Dakotas meant the airline now had to have stewardesses for the first time, initially, but eventually a total of fourteen girls covered flights to Paris, Channel Islands, Cork, Manchester and Glasgow.

On 23rd May 1955 C.A.S. was renamed Cambrian Airways. On the same date a company D.H. Dove crashed at Fittham Reg No. G-AKS, killing the pilot Bob Carson. The plane was on a flight from Cardiff to Southampton and Paris and there were six passengers aboard, with the pilot the only fatality.

A new route to Nice from Cardiff and Bristol was started but was not financially viable and was dropped.

In November an order was placed for two Herons, and the order was increased to three later. These aircraft came into service in the spring of 1956 Reg. Nos: G-AOGO, G-AORJ and G-AOGU.

Cambrian was now becoming a big airline and this was recognised by B.E.A. who entered into a ten-year agreement with Cambrian, giving the Welsh Airline the traffic rights from Liverpool to the Channel Islands and from Manchester to Jersey via Cardiff and Bristol.

In 1957 Bristol received a new airport at Lulsgate, therefore Cambrian moved from Whitchurch to Lulsgate. Cambrian also began operating from Fairwood Common which had been opened as the Swansea Airport on 1st June 1956. The first flight was Heron G-AORJ for Jersey. In 1958 B.E.A. acquired a one third interest in Cambrian and at the Board meeting they decided on a fifteen per cent increase in operations for the future of Wales and West of England's services, but this didn't work because 1958 saw a dramatic downturn in travel business. It was so bad that Cambrian was forced to sell off its aircraft and make many of its staff redundant; they retained just one Rapide for the Cardiff and Bristol run. The company reported a loss of £102,380 for the year ending 31st December 1958.

1959 saw an improvement and a new chairman Mr John Morgan brought more energy into the company. At the same time Wing Commander Bill Elwin became

M.D. and B.E.A. came to the aid of Cambrian. The state airline leased to the company three Pionaires Reg. Nos: G-AHCZ, G-AGIP and G-ALXL at the cheap rate of £7 per flying hour. On March 2nd scheduled services were resumed from Liverpool to Jersey via Cardiff and Bristol and from Bristol to Southampton and Paris.

At the end of the year the Pionairs were purchased by Cambrian from B.E.A. and in addition two more were bought later Reg Nos: G-AMEV and G-AMJX, making a fleet of five. On 1st April 1960 Cambrian inaugurated the service to Belfast cancelled in the crisis of 1958, together with all the other destinations forfeited at that time.

Viscounts of Cambrian Airways.

In 1961 three more Pionairs were acquired from B.E.A. and a new airport having been opened in Cork, Cambrian introduced services there from London, Bristol and Cardiff. By the end of September they had increased its traffic by 34% over the same period of the year before (52,585 in 1960 and 70,632 in 1961).

In 1962 the company established their own engineering base to do the maintenance work previously done by B.E.A on 1st April 1962 from Cardiff and Bristol to Glasgow.

In 1963 B.E.A. gave more routes to Cambrian which they considered loss making. They were linking flights: Isle of Man with Belfast, Liverpool, Manchester and London. These routes now made Cambrian the second largest independent operator in the U.K, and to enable them to operate these routes, B.E.A. sold five Viscounts to them together with a lot of spares of the price of £750,000. 1962 saw Cambrian carry 1,777,341 passengers.

The airline started new routes to Nice, Rimini, and Valencia in co-operation with 'Hourmonts' the local travel agent. In 1963 Cambrian numbered 76 engineers, 36 pilots and 28 cabin staff. Following the acquisition of Viscounts, the Pionairs fleet was reduced to five. G-AGIP, G-AMJX and G-AMFV being sold. The last named found its way to Gibraltar Airways with whom it flew the shuttle to Tangier, logging 10,558 crossings, before being replaced on 30th March 1970.

In 1965 three more Viscounts were bought making the fleet to eight, but G-AMOL carrying freight only, crashed at Speke airport. The runways were still not long enough for modern jets and the company could not compete with the likes of Luton or Gatwick.

1966 saw the purchase of five more Viscounts from Channel Airways at a cost of £750,000. The first six months of 1966 was a record period for Cambrian with 350,000 passengers on scheduled services (35% more).

1967 saw Cambrian needing more capital and it turned to B.E.A. for help, but help was also needed by another independent airline named B.K.S. form the north east of England who were in the same situation as Cambrian. British European Airways needed both companies to service and service their local communities so they encouraged the two companies to merge but in their own identities.

1968 saw the last Dakota flights from Paris to Rhoose to be sold. The Viscount fleet was now twelve strong and Pionairs numbered five. 1968 saw the departure of Wing Co. Bill Elwin. He resigned as Managing Director in March after 18 years with the company because he could see that Cambrian was losing its identity as the only truly Welsh airline. His job was shared by Mr Jim Callan and Mr David Davies , both becoming joint General Managers.

Captain de Wilde retired after eighteen years service. When he had joined in 1950 the airline had three pilots and on his departure pilots numbered one hundred and fifty three. The 31st October saw the last flights of the Pionairs. They were retired and Cambrian became a fleet of eleven Viscounts.

In 1968 British Eagle, one of Cambrian's rivals collapsed, and within twelve hours Cambrian took over their operation of Liverpool to Glasgow and Liverpool to London routes. It was a tough world for independent companies.

1969 saw the engineering based at Rhoose become the maintenance base for all British Air Services. This was then named Airways Engineering. B.A.S. was the title of the group formed by British European Airways to keep B.K.S. and Cambrian alive. B.E.A. did not want the routes that were serviced by the independents, as they knew that they would be unprofitable, so it was in their best interest o encourage them. A holding company was formed, called British Air Services which was 70% owned by B.E.A. B.A.S. then acquired 100% interest in both Cambrian and B.K.S. which was renamed North-Eastern Airlines. In December the first of Cambrian's B.A.C. I-II's was obtained from Autair.

The B.K.S. side of the partnership was losing money fast so in an attempt to stem the flow, Jim Callan was sent from Rhoose after twenty years' service to Hounslow to work for B.K.S. The new sole Managing Director at Rhoose was David Davies.

In a very eventful year at this growing airport 1970 saw the long awaited extension to what was to be the main runway (13/31) to a length of 7,000 feet for the introduction of jets. The Barry to Llantwit Major road had to be diverted to miss the southern extension of the runway. The work cost £5 million and was to be ready for the International rugby match between Ireland and Wales. Cambrian and Aer Lingus used Viscounts, B.A.C. I-II's and Boeing 737s put on 168 extra flights to fly approximately 7,000 Welsh supporters to Dublin. Other users of this runway were the Comets of Dan-Air that were used for Holiday Charters. Court Lines B.A.C I-II's, British Midlands using Viscounts and Heralds. To go with the new runway was a new technical block, and a fine Control Tower at the northeast boundary were built. In November 1969 a service between Cardiff and London was inaugurated, providing a link between South Wales and the rest of the world, but 1969 saw the end of some routes. In September the service from Swansea to Dublin and Jersey were withdrawn, and in the same month the Cardiff to Dinard service came to an end.

The company had bought its first B.A.C. I-II in December 1969. Five more were bought of which were Reg. Nos: G-AVOE, G-AVOF, G-AVGP. Cambrian had a new chairman Mr George T. Cantlay and they decided to go into the holiday charter business. The company was named Cambrian Holidays and took up agreements with the holiday agents Hourmont. Trips to Arenal, Benidorm and Torremolinos became frequent. On 1st April Cambrian began a service to Dubrovnic in Croatia (then Yugoslavia) which was formerly a B.E.A. route.

Operationally Cambrian was split into two fleets (on the bases) and Capt. Ken Wakefield was made Fleet Captain of I-II's, with Captain Ash Goodhew Fleet Captain Viscounts (Liverpool based). 1973 saw the start of a service to Lyon five times weekly with B.A.C. I-II's. Significantly in 1974 were the mergers between B.E.A. and B.O.A.C. which also included B.A.S. so now Cambrian became an integral part of British Airways, as the new state airline was called. On 1st April the name of Cambrian finally disappeared, when the company's staff, planes and equipment was

British Airways before they pulled out of Cardiff.

absorbed into British Airways. Despite its cash problems, it was a successful company, flying the flag of Wales for forty years. B.A.S. merged into B.E.A. Birmingham and B.E.A. Jersey to become British Regional Airlines shortly after operations ceased in 1978.

British Airways pulled out of Cardiff at least as far as scheduled service were concerned on 1st April 1980. British Regional had gradually built up a feeder service in and out of Cardiff.

On the departure of Cambrian, the engineering base at Cardiff was used by the parent, until they too left. These facilities at the old Cambrian base were taken over by British Air Ferries, where they designed and built an aircraft. A two-seat microlight. The prototype reg. G-MMAA first flew on 8th July 1982, and was to sell for £4,000. British Air Ferries suffered many set backs, and when new management took over, they not only abandoned the aircraft, but the engineering base as well.

Norman Aeroplane Co. (the result of a split in the famous Britten-Norman Co.) moved into Rhoose to a fine new hangar - workshop behind the old T2 hangar in 1986.

N.A.C. were to produce crop dusters, and water bombers in the guise of the "Fieldmaster". A fine trainer in the Firecracker, and a four-seat tourer named Freelance. They were all good designs, but the competition ensured that the N.A.C. failed shortly after they began serious production and vacated the site by 1990.

There were many other companies plying their services from Cardiff, including Dan-Air operated from Rhoose from the late fifties through to the mid-seventies, operating the Cardiff to Liverpool and Newcastle route. They also inaugurated flights to Norway, Holland, Belgium and the Isle of Man. They struggled, and like many other smaller airlines, they vanished from the regional airports.

The 1970's saw the holiday flying boom with the advent of the Court line, coupled with the local travel agency Hourmont. Clarkson, the brightly painted B.A.C. 1-11's were to be seen regularly at Rhoose until this company too crashed.

Brittania Airways continues to operate as it has done since the 1960's taking holiday makers to Spain, Canaries, Greece and Turkey. Airtours have also had a large and continuing interest in Cardiff since the company was formed. Channel Airways was a regular operator from Rhoose, mostly charter, and all inclusive tour flights.

Currently the airport is owned by the investment company T.B.I. and they have named their airport Cardiff International Airport. This is the last of an interminable list of names this place has endured since its opening in the fifties. When the Ministry of Transport and Civil Aviation ran it, it was merely Rhoose Airport. In 1965 it was acquired by Glamorgan County Council who reasonably name named it Glamorgan (Rhoose) Airport. Then in 1978 it became Cardiff (Wales) Airport.

It is international in so far as K.L.M. do five flights daily to Amsterdam. British Regional Airways operate from Cardiff to Belfast, Edinburgh, Glasgow and Aberdeen. To the continent they fly to Paris, Brussels and Guernsey. Manx offer twice daily flights to Jersey from here.

Since April 2000 the company Air 2000 has had a base operating at Cardiff, with a staff of seventy and full cabin staff and aircrew facilities at the excellent David's Hotel at Cardiff Bay. Monarch, Air Europa, Britannia, Spanair, Cyress Airways - all the usual carriers one would expect at a mid size airport are to be seen.

A weekly Boeing 747 flight to Orlando Florida operated by Airtours is established here. T.B.I. who own Cardiff International bought Belfast Airport in 1996, Orlando (Sanford) in 1997 and Skavst (Sweden) in 1988 and are currently looking for the council's approval for expansion in the Business Park outside the airfield. The Chairman of the company is a local man and the latest acquisition is Prestwick Airport.

The latest operator from Cardiff is Direct Holidays. With a ten million pound investment here they intend to do a lot of business from Cardiff and have com-

Concorde at Cardiff.

menced with 200 sunseekers to Salou. From April 2000 they will use destinations that include Spain, the Canaries and Greece for 2000 and a 43% increase for the year 2001. The management of Cardiff International is pleased with Direct Holidays' plans for the future as it will take Cardiff's capacity over the 1.5 million an increase of 21% on summer 1999. Direct Holidays intend to run a busy Winter Schedule as well as an expanding Summer programme in competition with Thomson, Airtours First Choice, J.M.C., Cosmos and bmiBaby.

The evolution of the airfield itself was a gradual process. Before 1970, the main runway as the NE to SW 03/21 which had been extended in the improvements of 1944 to 4,534 feet length, but it was impractical to extend further for the modern heavy jets coming into use, but the other subsidiary was. This was the NW - SE 13/31 runway. It has been extended from 3,000 ft to 3,700 ft since its R.A.F. days. It could be lengthened to 7,000 ft. By 1990 this was built at 7,732 ft x 151 ft. Glamorgan county was in fact a triumverate of the West, Mid and South Glamorgan County Councils who had come together to decide whether they needed an airport in South Wales, and if so where would it be sited. It was also agreed that the three Councils would fund deficits in the running of the airport chosen. Rhoose was the choice.

Cardiff International Airport in 1980.

Taking their combined ownership very seriously, the extensions, and taxi-ways were completed and a new Terminal was built on the opposite side of the airfield to the one where Cambrian used the annexe running along the side of the T2 hangar. With the terminal came a new Air Traffic Control tower and Meteorological Office. This cost the three authorities £5,000,000.

The new Meteorological Office was installed in an ideal, exposed site in the NW corner of the field with the instrument enclosure adjacent. This meteorological office was at Llandow airfield until 1954, transferring to the old R.A.F. site at Rhoose in April of 1954. This office not only provides advice to the flying aspect of the area, but provides the general public of Wales with its forecasts.

Rhoose is 67 metres above mean sea level. It is 1,500 metres inland from the Bristol Channel. With the Welsh mountains rising from about 15 kilometers to the north.

On the old R.A.F. site to the South of the main runway is situated Cardiff Flying

118

Aero-Club at Rhoose.

club and flying school, and a helicopter school run by Heli-Air Ltd. The old T2 hangar that had been brought from Withybush houses the privately owned planes and those of the clubs. The T2 has at some time beyond the memory of anyone employed there now, has had its original door gantries replaced with gantries of a Calender Hamilton. This hangar was condemned in 2002 and was demolished later that year.

The end of August 2000 saw the the start of a new airline at Cardiff. Air Wales launched a new Cardiff to Cork flight three times a week and a Cardiff to Stansted in a mid September slot. There are also plans for Manchester and either Newcastle or Sheffield. The airline will be based at Cardiff International and Swansea's fairwood Common and using a Donier 228 leased from Islanflug in Iceland with a letter of intent to take two more.

The airline is in discussion with Pembrey, Haverfordwest and Swansea to serve the West Wales area. A round Wales service is being studied. The Chairman of Air Wales, is Capt. John Howard Evans, who set up Brymon Airways, Paramount, and European Air Charter, in the U.K. and airlines in the Carribean. He was managing director of the original Air Wales in the 1970s which was taken over by Air U.K.

The managing director is David Smith, who was the sales director of Viking International an aircraft charter broker that took over Unijet and is now part of First Choice Holidays.

The British Airways Maintenance Hangar at Cardiff.

I was fortunate to be invited to an employee's family open day at this fine establishment in October 2000. It is located at the northern end of Cardiff International Airport. This hangar is devoted to the repair and service of B.A.'s considerable fleet of Boeing 747 and 777 aircraft.

The hangar has three bays, two of which are dedicated to 747's and the third can

1986 configuration for Cardiff International Airport. (PRU RAF 0959 18/6/86)

The British Airways Maintenance Hangar at Cardiff International Airport.

accommodate either the 747 or 777. The system of berthing these giants, involves towing the aircraft into a pre-positioned mark so that the nose is introduced into a shaped slot in the second floor of the hangar. This is named the Mezzanine floor and it extends the full length of the building, with an area of 6000 square metres, It has the width of a wide road, extending from the back wall of the hangar to the leading edge of the wing of the aircraft at its root. The level of this floor is just beneath the cabin doors when the plane is supported on its support with the centre-line level.

When the scaffolds and walkways have enclosed the length of the fuselage, and both wings are also surrounded by scaffolds, the huge structure that envelopes the tail assembly is swung around from left and right with the work staging to allow every foot of the tall vertical stabiliser to be examined.

The ground floor has pits for the retraction of the massive undercarriages, and the engines are worked on at this level, and the engine pylons, which provide a regular chore. The underside of the wings and fuselage are worked on from the ground, and the wings have their own workways. Well off the ground, but safe on rigid scaffolds that are sloping with the dihedral of the wing, work on ailerons and flaps can be carried out.

This impressive place was opened by The Prince of Wales in June 1993. There are 800 employees and approximately 100 contractors on site on a permanent basis. These are the systems specialists and technicians. The front of the hangar has a large apron that often holds two or three jumbos that are waiting their turn.

Because some aircraft do not need the full facilities of the hangar interior, a nose-in facility has been built on to the eastern end of the hangar at mezzanine level enabling lots of internal work to be done without taking up space inside. At the other end of the building some distance away outside on the apron, is the engine run-up bay.

The whole site occupies seventy acres, the hangar floor area is 22,000 square metres. The mezzanine area is 6000 square metres, and the support and administration buildings at the rear of the building has an area of 16,000 square metres.

The total weight of steel is 6,000 tonnes, the main spine beam is 1,000 tonnes, and the doors spine beam weighs 525 tonnes.

Overall length of beams = 244 metres
Depth of hangar   = 90 metres
Highest point of hangar = 33 metres

It was designed to withstand winds of 100 mph and the site has 600 car park spaces.

British Airways Fleet at November 2000.

	Model 136	Model 236	Model 436
Length	232 ft	232ft	232ft
Wingspan	195 ft	195 ft	211ft
Max take off weight	734,000lbs	820,000 lbs	870,000 lbs
Engines	P&W JT9D-7	RB 211-524 D4	RB 211-524H
T.O. Thrust	45500 lbs/eng	53100 lbs/eng	60600 lbs/eng
Max useable fuel	39,309 galls	44850 galls	47718 galls
B.A. seat config Main checks	376	373	383
Inter	5750 hrs	6250 hrs	6250 hrs
Major	24,000 hrs/ 5 yrs	24,000 hrs/ 5 yrs	24,000 hrs/ 5 yrs
Fleet comprises = 57	15	16	26

There are 37 on order, plus 26 options. By the end of year 2000 max fleet approx 104 if all 436's are delivered and al 136's are phased out.

The latest development at Cardiff International is the probable building of what is being termed as a centre of excellence in the aviation repair industry. D.A.R.A (Defence Aviation Repair Agency) after a long look at the ageing infrastructure at its Headquarters at St Athan, has decided to move the greater part of this operation to a site across the runway to the British Airways repair hangar.

The Welsh Development Agency has unveiled a blue-print that would put the current 2,500 employees at the heart of this new initiative.

Other jobs would be crated by a cluster of other aerospace firms attracted by D.A.R.A and British Airways Maintenance. The proposed complex would be sited opposite B.A. but consists of lower buildings than the B.A. facility to combat any environmental objections. It is believed that the move from St Athan would not entail the station closing completely, but that part of the work-load that utilised the regular flying aspect of the airfield such as the runway, which has caused some trepidation for many years at the old R.A.F station would be better served at Cardiff International Airport.

The vast workshops at St Athan and other facilities there would still retain some engineers. After all the two airfields are but a couple of miles apart. This was the situation in April 2001. This plan is no longer true. D.A.R.A. is to stay at St. Athan where a new hangar is to be built, and other changes will also be made.

By now there is little evidence of these small airfields, and the thrills that they supplied to the public in this new form of transport and of fighting wars. The hangars and other R.A.F. buildings of 52 M.U are still to be seen there, although refurbished in different materials to the originals. The airfield itself at Pengam Moors is mostly covered in a new housing estate, together with the ubiquitous Tesco store occupying the south of the old aerodrome, where men leaned their trade of war, and airshows in peacetime entertained us all.

The sea was that was to form the perimeter of the airfield can still be traced, and it was from here in the couple of summers before the outbreak of World War II that my friends and I, after cycling down from north Cardiff would view the activities on sunday mornings of the week-end pilots of No. 614 (County of Glamorgan) Auxiliary Air Force, fly their hawker Hinds, and Hectors. the aircraft were still in silver finish, and polished metal engine cowlings, and would dazzle when seen in the sun.

The company of John Curran and its factory no longer exists, neither does Air Dispatch. I must say that the finest coachwork on any buses or trolley buses on the Cardiff Corporation service were those built by Air Dispatch and its off-shoot Bruce Coachworks.

Ely Racecourse is now a leisure facility with many football pitches, the same can be said for the Glider field which is also football orientated partly, but also contains a leisure centre with a swimming pool. The Camp Heath cub strip is exactly as it was in 1944. Wenvoe is to most people, merely the place where the massive T.V. mast is sited high up on its plateau, they find it hard to believe that it was for a short time Cardiff's only functioning aerodrome, and that airshows performed here. Cardiff Flying Club was formed here, and 614 squadron practiced their army co-operation skills on this place - dropping and picking up messages a few feet off the ground.

Following on from this research will be a book describing the activities and histories of all forty-two airfields of Wales known to me - military and civil, large and small. This publication will be published with the aid of the works of aviation historians such as: Mr. David J. Smith, Mr. Aldon P. Ferguson, Mr. Roy Sloan, Mr. Roger Thomas, Mr. Edward Doylerush, Mr. Medwyn parry, and most importantly the endeavours of Mr. Derrick Elliot of the Central Register of Air Photographs for Wales.

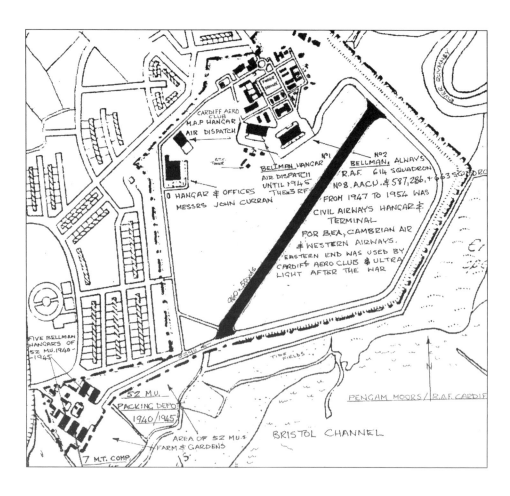

52 M.U. Pengam Moors, three years after closure. August 1948
(Welsh Assembly Government Photographic Unit)

Pengam Moors Airfield on 14th May 1950. 52 M.U. is to the south west. J. Curran is to the north west
with one of the Air Dispatch hangars above. The other hangars are to the north east
(Welsh Assembly Government Photographic Unit)

Pengam Moors. 1951

Pengam Moors. 1951

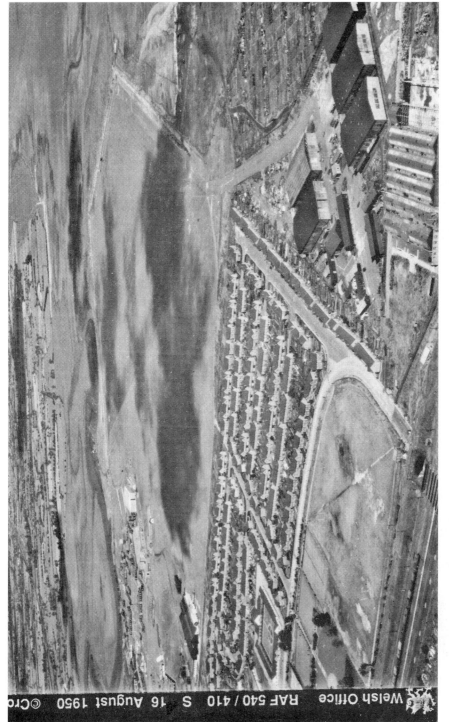

Pengam Moors from the West. The five Bellman hangars of 52 MU are visible on the bottom right of the picture. Courtesy of the Welsh Assembly.

RAF Cardiff - Civil Airport. 25th April 1952. Courtesy of the Welsh Assembly.